EDMUND

PICKENS

(OKCHANTUBBY)

FIRST ELECTED CHICKASAW CHIEF, HIS LIFE AND TIMES

BY JUANITA J. KEEL TATE

The Chickasaw Press

Edmund Pickens

Photo Courtesy of the Chickasaw Nation Photo Archives

CONTENTS

ACKNOWLEDGEMENTS

I t has been a great pleasure to accumulate these pages about my dear, respected great-grandfather, Edmund Pickens. Along the way, I received the crucial assistance of many people, without whom this book could not have been completed. I would like to take this opportunity to recognize many of these people.

Like any proud mother, I would like to begin with my children. It was my son Charles Guy Tate who first accompanied me to the old Chickasaw Nation territories east of the Mississippi River. My daughter, Gwendolyn Tate Gentry, and her daughters, Jennifer Gentry Lewis and Paula Gentry Klewer, also traveled with me across the former Chickasaw Nation. My oldest grandson Karl (Rudy) Boland accompanied me to northwest Alabama, Nashville, Tennessee and on to the town of Abbeville, South Carolina, the former home of Edmund Pickens' father, John Pickens. My niece, Yvonne Cannon, also toured Mississippi with me. My grandson, Jerod Impichchaachaaha' Tate, accompanied me through the former Chickasaw Nation three times, documenting everything in detail using photography and video.

Many thanks go to Dr. Forrest Tutor and Dr. Janis Tutor, as well as their sons. They are the current residents of Lochinvar, the former home of Molly Colbert, the grandmother of Chickasaw Governor Cyrus Harris. My thanks for the hospitality of the citizens of Pontotoc, Mississippi and for the assistance of Hazel Boss Neet, former chancery clerk of Pontotoc County. Ms. Neet's knowledge of Chickasaw records during the era of the Great Removal was remarkable and invaluable. Hearty appreciation is also extended to Ann and Ben Craig, who escorted me to the bridge overlooking the site of the Natchez Trace and let me stay in their home during my visit to the Festival of Singing River, attended by members of the Choctaw, Cherokee, Creek tribes and others.

I owe my sincere gratitude to Betty Griffith of Ardmore, Oklahoma for rendering extensive reading assistance for nearly 18 months; also to Etta Postoak Johnson for assisting with reading and library research in my home library; and to Vickie Luster and Faye Orr for their aid in research at the Chickasaw Council House Museum in Tishomingo, Oklahoma.

In the last several years, my cousin Kathleen Stoner of Duncan, Oklahoma, has been of enormous help concerning the Pickens line of our family. In addition, I was greatly assisted by Mary Jane Lowery of Madill, Oklahoma, Frank Potts, John Cobb and his daughter, Dr. Amanda Cobb-Greetham.

My mother, Lula Potts Keel, told wonderful stories to me when I was a child. They ranged from personal experiences to tales of her half-sister, Sophia Fry Reeder, and brother, Sam Fry, both of whom were orphaned at an early age. As a child, I was fascinated by my mother's stories. Little did I realize I would never forget those marvelous tales and one day compile many of them in a book. My mother taught all 10 of her children the importance of our history and to take pride in our heritage.

She taught us the surnames and family stories of the lines of my heritage – Pickens, Cravatt, Harris and Keel, along with other, far-removed families.

I would also like to thank my cousins, the Potts, Pratts, Willifords, Cobbs, Wooleys, Browns, McMillans and others. I am grateful for the words of encouragement you gave me to write this book.

I fondly salute my father, Guy Keel, whose first language was Chickasaw. Noting my tiny size due to premature birth, he gave me the Chickasaw name Foshi' (Little Bird). This name has remained with me my entire life, which now nearly spans a century. I am deeply proud of my Chickasaw heritage.

Last, but not least, my abiding gratitude goes to my grandson's (Jerod Impichchaachaaha' Tate's) wife, Ursula Running Bear, an enrolled member of the Rosebud Sioux Tribe (Sicangu Lakota), who typed and assisted in editing the first drafts of this book.

Acknowledgements

PREFACE

M y real inspiration to write this book began in the fall of 1961. In September of that year, my sister Minnie Keel Edwards and I took my son, Charles Guy Tate, to attend Union Theological Seminary in New York City. Minnie and I then drove to Washington, D.C. for a tour. While there, I visited the National Archives. It was at that point that I made one of the most important decisions of my life – to return to Washington, D.C. and begin studying and recording my genealogy. I became a member of the Ardmore Genealogy Society and the United Daughters of the Confederacy, and attended monthly meetings of the Choctaw and Chickasaw tribes. Along with long interviews of personal friends of my mother, Lula, all of these organizations helped me begin my genealogical research. And what a search it has been! As my mother had done, I passed much of my knowledge on to my children and grandchildren, who have dutifully retained it.

In 1979, I traveled to Oklahoma City and the Oklahoma Historical Society. Fortunately, the archivist of the Indian tribes, Ms. Rella Looney, was a Chickasaw. Upon learning of my interest in Edmund Pickens, she showed me a letter dated from a few years prior from the Reverend Eron M. Sharp of Memphis, Tennessee. In the letter, Reverend Sharp inquired about descendants of Edmund Pickens. Reverend Sharp was descended from a relative of Edmund Pickens' father, John Pickens, whose genealogy he had been researching in Mississippi. Quite a coincidence! Reverend Sharp and his wife, Alma, were very helpful as archivists, since he has served as pastor of several churches in Mississippi and knew many Pickens relatives. I corresponded with Reverend Sharp many times and began a long-standing friendship.

In 1980, my son, Charles Guy Tate, drove us to Memphis, Tennessee, and we enjoyed a fascinating visit of the old Chickasaw Nation. Beginning with a tour of Chucalissa Village, a restored Chickasaw village unearthed by students of Memphis State University, we toured the old Chickasaw Nation territory from Memphis to Florence, Alabama. We then traveled into Alabama, across the Tennessee River and across southern Tennessee (past a former home of the Edmund Pickens family), then back to Memphis and at last, home to Ardmore, Oklahoma.

After that, more of my genealogy trips began in earnest. The following are some of the sites I have been able to visit: the source of the Five Civilized Tribes' records in Muskogee, Oklahoma; the Oklahoma Historical Society in Oklahoma City; the Federal Records Center in Fort Worth, Texas and the nearby Dallas Public Library; the Ardmore Public Library, which is the meeting place of the Ardmore Genealogy Society; the Carter County Courthouse; county courthouses from the old Chickasaw and Choctaw Nations of Oklahoma; the homes of many elderly Choctaw and Chickasaw members; various Choctaw and Chickasaw meetings sites; the Chickasaw girls school, Carter Seminary (formerly Bloomfield Academy), where I was a student for a time; the Choctaw boy's school, known as Goodland, in Hugo, Oklahoma; and the Chilocco Indian School south of Arkansas City, Kansas, where I graduated in 1928. All of these institutions and personal contacts, including those of James and Elaine Colbert, and their daughter Tania Colbert Patrick, Marie Garland and Ella Jean Cary, a Chickasaw-Choctaw friend, were an enormous help.

As my interest increased, so did my research results. Information about people and places relating to my heritage poured in to me. Information regarding cemeteries that held the memories of my Pickens people, particularly my great-grandfather Edmund Pickens, came from all directions. I made many new friends, even among paternal relatives, whom my mother had known and only told me about. As I continually contacted these people, I was delighted to notice that they too were becoming more interested in our shared genealogy. Our research became so fascinating that we began to delve into our Scottish origins – for instance, Edmund Pickens' ancestor Robert Pickens, who had left the Scottish lowlands many years before.

In 1984, at a meeting of the Ohoyohoma Club (Indian Women Club), I announced that I would go to Scotland if I could get someone to accompany me. Edna Shoemaker, a Choctaw friend of mine, responded that she would gladly go. Within weeks, we were on our way. On that 17-day tour, we landed in central Ireland, and then traveled to eastern Scotland, as far north as Inverness on the North Sea. We were guided into western England and Wales to Stonehenge, and then back through Wales and London. In London, we were able to visit the largest bookstore in the city and purchase some rare books about Scotland. That ended our tour of Robert Pickens' ancestral home. Back in my birthplace of Ardmore, Oklahoma, I decided that these trips, with their wonderful experiences, would formulate a future book.

Shortly thereafter, I returned to Washington, D.C. to attend a genealogical session involving people from all over the country. I established many relationships, including some with Chickasaws and even my own relatives. It was in Washington, D.C. that I discovered the important position Edmund Pickens had held in our tribe. Even though my mother had been the teacher in our small Chickasaw school north of Lebanon, Chickasaw Nation, Indian Territory (I.T.), prior to her marriage to my father, none of my relatives' stories had gone farther back than a couple of generations. In particular, Edmund Pickens' history had never been documented.

Edmund Pickens was a man of the times. As the first and only elected Chickasaw Chief, he served well and honestly in tribal affairs while he reared a large family with his wife, Euthlike. Other tribal leaders often requested his presence during negotiations with the United States or when they had business with other tribes. Through the change of tribal government, he continued to serve his Chickasaw people and, at his death, left an unblemished reputation for integrity and dedication to the welfare of every tribal member. The name Edmund Pickens deserves a special place of honor and should be long remembered.

I hope that others will likewise share their knowledge about this great Chickasaw Chief, Edmund Pickens, whom I consider one of the finest characters in Chickasaw history.

Juanita J. Keel Tate

The Great Seal of the Chickasaw Nation Circa 1856

The Great Seal of the Chickasaw Nation came into being with Article 5, Section 10 and 11 of the Chickasaw Constitution of 1856.

The Great Seal of the Chickasaw Nation today

Oklahoma historian Murial Wright wrote about the Chickasaw Seal in 1940 saying that "the figure of the warrior ... commemorated the courageous Chickasaw of old times, represented in the person and character of Chief Tishomingo."

The Pickens Coat-of-Arms

He Beareth Arms: Found in Burke's General Armory, Scotland.
This resource catalogs all amorial bearings for Scotland, England and
Ireland from their origins to 1844.

Translated into non-Heraldic terms: A blue (azure) shield with six
silver (argent) plates arranged in rows of three, two and one, from top to
bottom. The demy-lion rampart issues from the wreath of the two main
colors of the shield – silver and blue.

The silver plates denote generosity. The demi-lion means the same as a
whole lion, which holds a high place in Heraldry as the emblem of courage.

The lion represents the image of a good soldier, who must be valiant
of courage, strong of body, polite in council and a foe to fear. It is the
emblem of St. Marks.

Colors are personal characteristics granted to the bearer only on merit.
Blue signifies loyalty; silver signifies sincerity and peace.

© Copyright 2008 The Chickasaw Press
ISBN 978-0-09797858-2-5

EDMUND
PICKENS

(OKCHANTUBBY)

FIRST ELECTED CHICKASAW CHIEF, HIS LIFE AND TIMES

JOHN PICKENS

C H A P T E R   O N E

Conflicts between countries are common and have often determined world history. The conflict between England and Scotland directly affected the Indian tribes of North America. During the seventeenth century, many Scottish people migrated to France and other countries to avoid the conflict between England and Scotland. During this time, Robert Pickens, a Scottish lowlander, made a personal decision that would greatly affect the Chickasaw Nation a century later. Young Robert Pickens migrated to Normandy, France, where he obtained work as a postal clerk and settled down with the intention of living there permanently. At that time, he could not know that a serious European event would change his plans completely.

Robert, a Protestant, met and married Mademoiselle Jeanne Bonneau, a devout French Huguenot. Although France was essentially a Catholic country, Robert and Jeanne were able to live a peaceful life due to the Edict of Nantes. The Edict of Nantes was issued on April 13, 1598, granting civil rights to the French Calvinists (Huguenots) and Presbyterians; however, in October 1685, Louis XIV, the grandson of Henry

IV, renounced the Edict and declared Protestantism illegal, with the Edict of Fontainebleau. This act, most commonly called the "Revocation of the Edict of Nantes," affected Robert and his family, so they moved to Limerick, Ireland, hoping for a more stable life.

In 1718, the Robert Pickens family left Limerick and sailed for the Colonies of North America. Robert's son, William, along with William's wife and children, arrived far north, in Bucks County, Pennsylvania, where they settled. Contrary to William's route, Robert, Jeanne and at least three of their sons preferred to take the southern route. They arrived in Charleston, South Carolina, where this gregarious family happily established a permanent home.

Through the years, the children of William Pickens moved to other colonies. His son, Robert Pike Pickens, continued southward during the latter half of the eighteenth century in what was then the Cherokee Nation. Robert Pike Pickens, his wife Miriam and their children found a permanent home in the small, but

Revolutionary soldier, Brigadier General Andrew Pickens, a cousin of Robert Pike Pickens, was the executioner of, and a signatory to, the treaty with the Cherokee people, known as the Treaty of Hopewell, signed on November 28, 1785.

*Francis Wilkinson
Pickens (1805 - 1869),
another cousin of Robert
Pike Pickens.*

*(Harper's Weekly Journal of
Civilization, January 9, 1861,
Vol. V. – No. 212.)*

very active community of Abbeville, South Carolina. Robert's cousin John Pickens helped establish the Cherokee Nation line north of the Pickens' home. He later became friends with the nationally known John Calhoun of the same area.

✸

Pickens is a respected name appearing on the maps of practically all of the southern states. The Pickens family name adorns towns, counties, roads and creeks. Pickens District is one of the four districts in the Chickasaw Nation of Oklahoma. There are many descendants of Robert Pickens who had a significant role in shaping the United States of America.

Revolutionary soldier, Brigadier General Andrew Pickens, a cousin of Robert Pike Pickens, was the executioner of, and a signatory to, the treaty with the Cherokee people, known as the Treaty of Hopewell, signed on November 28, 1785.

Francis Wilkinson Pickens (1805 - 1869), another cousin of Robert Pike

Pickens, served as a member of the U.S. House of Representatives from 1834 - 1843 and was appointed Ambassador to Russia by President James Buchanan. After returning from Russia, he was elected Governor of South Carolina at the outbreak of the Civil War.

Alabama's third governor, Israel Pickens, still another cousin of Robert Pike Pickens, was a native of North Carolina. He served in the North Carolina Senate from 1808 - 1810, represented North Carolina in the U.S. House of Representatives from 1811 - 1817 and represented the "North Carolina Faction" in early Alabama politics. He was active in the American Colonization Society, was interested in scientific research and invented a lunar dial. Israel Pickens was appointed to the U.S. Senate and retired to Cuba, due to ill health, where he died on April 24, 1827.

Alabama's third governor, Israel Pickens.

(Alabama Department of Archives and History)

Many early American colonists of the Carolinas, Georgia, Tennessee and Virginia became well acquainted with their neighboring Indian tribes. Dozens of friendships ripened into marriages; however, the Robert Pike Pickens family did not prefer this close association. Yet, Robert's sons, John and David, often visited Cherokee friends, much to the consternation of their parents. The Cherokee trail to Atlanta lay only a few miles from the Pickens home near Abbeville, and it was inevitable that the gregarious sons would develop Cherokee friendships. Robert did not understand this, since there was a great deal of enmity that existed between them and the Cherokee people.

In 1761, Cherokees in the Abbeville vicinity burned Joseph Pickens, a cousin to John Pickens, at the stake. The Pickens family was justifiably outraged. Suspicious of his Cherokee relationships, John's family accused him of being involved. John vowed his innocence, but it was to no avail. Thereafter, his name became anathema to all his relatives except his younger brother David and his sister. John endured these accusations for some time; however, this tragic event ultimately led to an irrevocable change in his life. One last time at a family gathering, John proclaimed his innocence, but he still refused to break ties with his Cherokee friends.

One morning in 1786, John Pickens looked out of his window at the road leading to the Cherokee Trail, where he could see traders and other travelers heading west. Where they were going was no mystery, and John needed no explanation for this heavy amount of traffic. John's mind was made up – he would soon be joining them. Bidding David farewell, he took to his horse, which was laden with the few possessions he could carry with him. John was deeply hurt by his family's accusations and soon joined the traders on their westward journey.

Within weeks, he arrived in the Creek Nation. Being unfamiliar there, he traded fresh horses and continued on to the Choctaw Nation in Mississippi. There he found his old friends, who welcomed him. Exhausted, John accepted their invitation to remain as long as he desired, although the growing town of Natchez was more appealing. At that crossroads of heavy traffic, which he considered "back home," he reminded himself that there would be many business opportunities. Having grown up in a family involved with livestock, he felt good about this line of business. With gratitude for the hospitality of his Choctaw friends, John soon left the Choctaw Nation and traveled to Natchez.

The Natchez Trace was a 444-mile trade route that cut completely through the Chickasaw Nation from Natchez to Nashville, Tennessee. Several inns (or "stands")

Colbert's Stand is located on the Natchez Trace in Alabama.

(Courtesy of the Natchez Trace Parkway, U.S. National Park Service.)

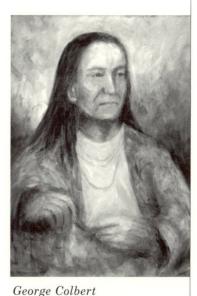

George Colbert

(Courtesy of the Natchez Trace Parkway, U.S. National Park Service.)

were set up along the trail that offered a respite for travelers. A Chickasaw, George Colbert, operated the most prominent of these stands at the junction of the Natchez Trace and the Tennessee River. It was there that he reportedly charged General Andrew Jackson $75,000 to ferry his army across the river. While this angered the General at the time, it was a common demonstration of tribal autonomy and Indian nationalism in early America.

Located at the southernmost point of the heavily traveled Natchez Trace, and with its connection to the abundant river traffic, John Pickens envisioned a prosperous life there. The industrious and friendly John Pickens met many people in Natchez, and within days became acquainted with many business people. After only a few weeks, John had an active livestock business partnership with Richard King of Natchez. Advantageously located in the center of town, the business did well. It was in Natchez that John met and married a Chickasaw woman named Mary.

On January 18, 1789, John became seriously ill while work-ing with his livestock adjoining the home of his business partner, Richard King. (Diagnosis of John's sudden illness is documented in later court records.) John was removed to Richard King's home, and a messenger boy was immedi-ately sent to get Mary at the Pickens home. It is clear that John realized his illness would be terminal. Within a few hours, he drafted a will that left his property to Mary, their expected child, and John's youngest brother, David, who had remained in Abbeville. The soon-to-be-born child of John and Mary Pickens was Edmund Pickens, a name that would become historically significant to the Chickasaw Nation.

The will of John Pickens was probated in Natchez, and the records of the office of the chancery clerk reveal the following documents:

WILL

IN THE NAME OF GOD AMEN: I, John Pickens, of the District of Natchez, being weak in body but of sound and perfect mind and memory (blessed by God for the same), considering the mortality of my body, and knowing that it is appointed for all men once to die, do make and publish this my last will and testament in the manner and form following (that is to say) first: I resign my body to the Dust from which it came and my soul into the hand of God, who gave it; and as for what worldly Estate it has pleased God to give me, I dispose of it in the following manner: first: that all my just debts and funeral charges shall be paid: and the remainder to be divided equally into three parts of which I give one third to my beloved wife Mary; one third to the child that my said wife is now pregnant with, and the remaining one third I give to my brother David Pickens; and for the full performance of the same, I do appoint my trusty and worthy friends Robert Miller and Charles Collins of the District aforesaid, Executors to this my last Will and Testament. In witness whereof I have hereunto set my hand and affixed my seal this eighteenth day of January in the year of our Lord, one thousand seven hundred and eighty nine.

J. Pickens (Seal)

Signed, sealed and delivered in the presence of Richard King – Jn. Griffing – John Bell – Justus King – Prosper King – Oswell X (his mark) Yarbrough.

In Natchez on this twenty second day of the month of January in the year one thousand seven hundred and eighty nine, before me, Don Carlos de Grand Pre, Lieutenant Colonel in the Royal Armies and Civil and Military Commandant of the said Port and District appeared Richard Miller, who informed me of the death of John Pickens, who died on the eighteenth day of the present month at the house of Justus King, to which he had removed by reason of sickness, intending to make a Journey to the Choctaw Towns; and thereupon the said Miller delivered to me the sealed will of the said Pickens and the witnesses who signed the same being also present I proceeded immediately to open the said Will in the presence, namely: Richard King, John Griffing, John Bell, Justus King, Prosper King and Oswell Yarbrough, all of who being duly sworn were asked if the signature purporting to be that of the deceased Pickens was really his own writing and the signatures following were really their own. To which they answered that the signatures of Pickens was really his own writing, and the others they acknowledged to be their own, ratifying and confirming the same, in the presence of Don Antonio Soler, Don Joseph Martinez Rubio and Juan Carreras, Witnesses present – Richard King – Justus King – John Bell – Jn. Griffing – Oswell X (his mark) Yarbrough – Prosper King – Jose Martinez Rubio – Antonio Soler – Juan Carrerras – Estevan Maiar – Interpr. Carlos de Grand Pre.

At the Port of Natchez on this twenty sixth day of the month
of January in the year one thousand seven hundred and eighty
nine, I Don Carlos de Grand Pre, Lieutenant Colonel in the
Royal Armies, and Civil and Military Commandant of the said
Port and District, accompanied by the Interpreter, the Executor of the Will, and the Partner of the deceased, repaired to
the House of Richard Adams, in which the Widow of the said
decease John Pickens resides, who I required to declare all and
every property in her possession belonging to her deceased husband, as likewise the Cattle and horses if any, in order that an
inventory thereof may be taken of the whole Estate, in which
I have proceeded as follows. – Two shirts. Two pairs trousers.
Two pair pantaloons of cotton. One pair cloth Ditto. 1 Cotton vest. 2 roundabouts ditto. One old cloth Great-coat. One
pair large breeches, old. One old hat. One saddle. Cattle and
horses, vz: Several horses running in the Woods, branded with
the brand of the deceased. And there being nothing more to Inventory, I have closed this present sitting and have signed with
the said Widow, the Executors, the Interpreter, and Witnesses
assisting. – Robert Miller – Antonio Soler - Franc Pabana

Her

Mary M.P. Pickens

Mark

-- Carlos de Grand Pre --

At the said Plantation at two p.m., finding that the Partner of the decease had in his possession all the Papers yea. Relating to the affairs of the deceased, have closed the Inventory for the present and have signed with the Widow, the Executors, the Interpreter and witnesses assisting.

Her

Mary M.P. Pickens

Mark

Robert Miller – Franco Pabana – Juan Carreras – Antonio Soler – Grand Pre.

At the Port of Natchez on this twenty seventh day of the month and year before written, I the said Commandant, accompanied by the Interpreter and Witnesses assisting, have repaired to the House of Richard Adams, to continue the Inventory, and not finding Richard King there, who has in his possession all the papers belonging to the deceased, the said Inventory could not be continued; whereupon I have closed this present sitting, and have signed with the Widow the Interpreter, and the Witnesses assisting.

Robert Miller – Juan Carreras – Antonio Soler – Grand Pre.

At the Port aforesaid on this twenty-sixth day of the month and year before written, I the said Commandant, have repaired to the Plantation of Richard King who has in his charge sundry horses and mares belonging to him and the deceased John Pickens in partnership, as also sundry notes given by individuals for horses sold and have proceeded in the Inventory thereof, in presence of the Interpreter and Witnesses assisting as follows:

Ten horses running in the cane marked one half 3 P and the others as a▽. Twenty mares running also in the cane marked in the same manner. Five Colts, in the same range, branded in the same manner. Seven horses on the other side of the River, branded in the same manner. Eight mares running in the same range, branded in the same manner. Thirty-five horses and mares at the Aroyelles branded in the same manner. One horse on the Plantation of Richard Adams, branded in the same manner. Two mares and one Colt at the same place, branded in the same manner. One horse said to have been stolen by Herman Kirk and Samuel Walker. And it being noon, I have closed this present sitting and there being no more horses to inventory, I have signed with the Widow, the Executor, the Interpreter, and Witnesses assisting. Richard King, Juan Carreras, Franco Pabana, Robert Miller, Grand Pre.

Four days after John's death, Robert Miller, one of the Executors of his will, informed the magistrate, Don Carlos de Grand Pre, Lieutenant Colonel in the Royal Armies and

Juanita Keel Tate in front of the home of Richard King, now known as the Post House.

Civil and Military Commandant of the said Port and District. Thereupon, his will was duly probated beginning January 22, 1789. As noted on previous pages, John Pickens' estate was inventoried in the required manner, in the presence of Mary, his widow, whom they contacted at the home of Richard Adams, where she and John had been living at the time of his death. Witnesses and assistants in the procedure were Don Antonio Soler, Don Joseph Martinez Rubio, Juan Carreras, Richard and Justus King, John Bell, John Griffings, Oswell Yarbrough and Prosper King. Interpreter was Estevan Maiar. (Before the magistrate) Carlos de Grand Pre.

The inventory consisted mostly of livestock, including horses, oxen, mares, and colts and was branded with one of these brands: "one half 3P" or "A▽." In addition, there was a small fortune in promissory notes payable to John Pickens. John's business partner, Richard King, reported many verbal notes payable to the deceased, which were added to inventory.

After the sale of livestock in February, April and June 1789, the estate of John Pickens was legally and satisfactorily closed, as acknowledged by his business partner, Richard King, on June 22, 1789. And so it was that a few months after his father's death in 1789, Edmund Pickens was born.

Editor's Note: Over a century later, descendants of Edmund Pickens, Juanita Keel Tate, Gwendolyn Tate Gentry, Paula Gentry Klewer and Jerod Impichchaachaaha' Tate visited the King home, now known as the "Post House," situated at the extreme south end of the Natchez Trace. They found the ground floor – formerly a stable – converted into an attractive restaurant, and toured the upper floors. One of the upstairs rooms is where John Pickens, Mrs. Tate's great-great grandfather, executed his last will and testament before passing away.

The table on the following page lists several of the author's ancestors:

Abstracts of Locations made under the 6th Article of the Treaty with the Chickasaws the 24th day of May, 1834, by Col. Benjamin Reynolds, Indian Agent, and the Chiefs of the Chickasaw Nation.

Number	Names of Persons	Sex	Age	Quantity Entitled	Half or Fractional	Section	Township	Range	East or West	Remarks	District
30	Delila Thomas	Female	25	1		7	4	2	W		
53	Molly Gunn	Female	55	1		17	10	3	E		
100	Malcolm McGee	Male	75	1		21	12	3	E		
581	William Colbert	Male		1		33	2	10	W		
540	Jane Aldridge	Female		3½		30	3	13	W		
						31	3	13	W		
						36	3	13	W		
						14	3	13	W		
248	Levi Kemp	Male		3½	South ½ of	19	10	4	E		
						9	14	6	E		
						10	14	6	E		
						3	14	6	E		
314	Edmond Pickens			3		7	1	1	W		
						18	1	1	W		
						13	1	2	W		
315	Susan Guest			3		19	1	1	W		
						30	1	1	W		
						31	1	1	W		
317	Oni yea Thomas			4		23	1	1	W		
						22	1	1	W		
						15	1	1	W		
						24	4	4	W		
728	Isaac Alberson			3½	West ½ of	8	8	2	W		
						9	8	2	W		
						6	7	8	W		
						7	7	8	W		
895	Dickson Frazier			2		7	11	6	N		
						8	11	6	N		

GOING HOME

C H A P T E R   T W O

In accordance with the final conversation between John and Mary Pickens, Mary took their young son, Edmund, and returned to Chickasaw Nation territory. Natchez, although comfortable for the young couple, had become overrun by an influx of immigrants and was not the best place to raise a child. The Chickasaw Nation offered a safer, more stable and acceptable environment for the widow and her son.

"We are going home!" The anticipation increased as the miles rolled by under the wheels of the surrey bearing many of the possessions of the young mother and her infant. Mary's excitement knew no bounds as she anticipated seeing her cousins again and introducing them to young Edmund, the newest member of the Shawi' (Raccoon) Clan, the second highest clan in the Chickasaw tribe. Following her marriage to John Pickens, the young Chickasaw woman had never ceased to yearn for the place of her birth. The prospect of again hearing familiar conversations in the Chickasaw language was music to her ears. Mary noted the contrast between her beloved Chickasaw Nation and the hectic Mississippi River port of Natchez. Interesting and exciting as it was, Natchez was no match for

Chickasaw territory. It was there, at his mother's original home, that Edmund spent the next several decades of his life.

Little is known of the life of Edmund Pickens in the 29 years between his birth and 1818. We do know that he was given the Chickasaw warrior name Okchantubby, which translates to "he survived and killed." Present day descendants of Edmund Pickens continue to identify themselves as Shawi' Clan.

In the mid-1790s, Mary married Bernard McLaughlin in accordance with Chickasaw tribal customs. McLaughlin was a native of Scotland who settled in the Chickasaw Nation as an interpreter. They had several children whose names appear on the 1818 Chickasaw census: Barney, Katy, James, Becca, Betsey, Jacky, Aaron and Patrick. There is evidence that Edmund Pickens was very close to the McLaughlin children.

Edmund's name appears on this same 1818 Chickasaw census simply as "Edmund" in the Bernard McLaughlin family. (The 1818 Chickasaw census is discussed in more detail in *Chapter 3*.)

In later years, Edmund and James McLaughlin became leaders of the Chickasaw tribe. James began as an interpreter, following in his father Bernard's footsteps, and was eventually elevated to important roles during the Chickasaw removal to Indian Territory.

In 1823 the Presbyterian Synod sent Father Thomas C. Stuart to the Chickasaw Nation for the purpose of establishing a mission five miles south of Pontotoc, Mississippi. This new interracial Presbyterian mission was named Monroe Mission and opened on June 7, 1823. Father Stuart remained there many years, during which he kept detailed records, including names and dates of those who became members. These included many Chickasaw Indians, their slaves and other whites. Bernard McLaughlin and his family joined the mission. Edmund Pickens, his wife Euthlike (a.k.a., "Liney" or "Tiney") and their children Johnson, David, Rachel and Mary, also became members. Due to illegible handwriting, we still do not know the exact nickname of Euthlike – whether it was Liney or Tiney. The dates of membership of the Pickens family are on record with the Presbyterian Church denomination and can be found at the Pontotoc Public Library in Mississippi.

It is not known whether the Joseph B. Adams, whose notation appeared on the Session records dated October 24, 1829, was a relative of Richard Adams, with whom Mary and John Pickens were living in Natchez when John died. However, it is highly probable that he was a relative of Mary Pickens McLaughlin. He was at the little Pontotoc Mission when David Pickens, brother of John Pickens was serving as missionary farmer. According to Father Stuart's diary, Joseph Adams was also present on October 4, 1829, when Mrs. McLaughlin was baptized at Monroe Mission. Bernard McLaughlin was the first member of this family to become affiliated with Monroe Mission, according to the mission's records and Father Stuart's diary, which states:

> **Dec. 4th (1824).** *"Mr. Bernard McLaughlin, Mrs. Tennessee Bynum, a native, and Ester, a black woman belonging to Mrs. Colbert, having given satisfactory evidence of a work of grace upon their hearts, were admitted as members of the church. Ester was baptized."*

Dec. 25th 1825. *"The ordinance of baptism was adminis-tered to the three black people received on yesterday; also to Mr. McLaughlin's daughter, Susan."*

Oct. 2, 1829. *"The church session met and was constituted by prayer by Rev. Cyrus Byington. Mrs. Mary Gunn and Mrs. McLaughlin were examined with reference to church privileges and approved."*

Oct. 3, 1829. *"The session met according to adjournment and examined and approved Lewis and Cassander, people of color."*

October 4. *"Mrs. McLaughlin and Cassander, having assented to the requisite questions, were baptized by Rev. Cyrus Byington, and together with Mrs. Gunn and Lewis, for the first time received the Lord's Supper."* Joseph B. Adams.

April 3, 1830. *"Rev. Cyrus Byington conversed with the following persons with reference to the admission to the church, viz: Edmund Pickens, Sally Fraser, Nuzeka Col-bert, Dise Colbert, Betsey (Creek woman) and Amy and Syke, colored people. These persons appearing well, were on the Sabbath baptized and received into the church. W. H. Barr's infant daughter, Belinda, was baptized. At the monthly concert for prayer the Monday evening follow-ing, the sum of $14.68 was contributed for the spread of the gospel.*

(No date). *"Session met and was opened with prayer. Mrs. Liney Pickens, a native woman, presented herself for* *examination with a view to unite herself with the church. Her examination being very satisfactory, she was admitted. Concluded with prayer."*

May 1, 1831. *"The ordinance of baptism was administered to Mrs. Pickens, also (her husband being present) to her children, Rachel, Mary and David."*

~ THOMAS C. STUART Mod.

A few months later the oldest son, Johnson Pickens, was baptized. He had been visiting a cousin at the time the other family members were baptized.

As an adult, Edmund Pickens settled his family on the old Chickasaw Nation/Tennessee line, in Township 1 South, Range 1 West and Township 1 South, Range 2 West, adjoining Marshall County, Mississippi Territory. This land was situated 18 miles northeast of the little town of Holly Springs.

John Pickens' cousins settled in various areas of the southern states, including Mississippi and Tennessee. Some family members even resided a few miles to the north of Edmund's family, in Fayette County, Tennessee. They remained in close contact until the removal of the tribe to Indian Territory.

Plans for The Removal

C H A P T E R   T H R E E

As the American population increased in the United States, so did the demand for habitable lands. Gradual association of the colonists with Indian tribes brought about intermarriage of many Indians with non-Indians. Pressure from non-Indian settlers in the Mississippi Territory brought about demands for the tribes to relocate westward.

President Thomas Jefferson and other United States officials played an active part in making treaties with Indians and providing for a westward movement. The Louisiana Purchase was an excuse to completely remove Indians to that new territory in early 1803, and Thomas Jefferson's intentions were clearly articulated before that purchase:

> *"From the Yazoo to the Ohio is the property of the Chickasaw,*
> *a tribe the most friendly to us, and at the same time the most*
> *adverse to the diminution of their lands. The portion of their*
> *territory, of first importance to us, would be the slip between*
> *the Mississippi on the west, and on the east the Yazoo and the*

ridge dividing the waters of the Mississippi and the Tennessee. Their main settlements are east of this ... The method by which we may advance towards our object will be, to establish among them a factory or factories or furnishing them with all necessaries and comforts they may wish (spirituous liquors excepted), and encouraging these, and especially their leading men, to run in debt beyond their individual means of paying; and whenever in that situation, they will always cede lands to rid themselves of debt. A factory about the Chickasaw Bluffs would be tolerably central. We should continue to increase and nourish their friendship and confidence by every act of justice and of favor which we can possibly render them. What we do in favor of other Indians should not constitute the measure of what we do for these, our views as these being much more important. This tribe is very poor, and they want necessaries (with) which we abound. We want lands with which they abound, and these natural wants seem to offer fair ground of mutual supply."

~ Thomas Jefferson

(Samuel C. Adams. Beginnings of West Tennessee, Johnson City, Tennessee: Watauga Press, 1930, p.12.)

Thomas Jefferson, Author of the Declaration of Independence and Third U.S. President.

(Thomas Jefferson by Rembrandt Peale - Public Domain)

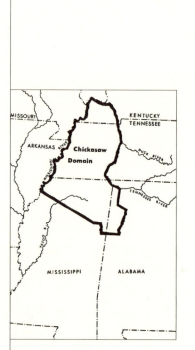

Ancient Chickasaw domain.

(Map from Arrell M. Gibson's The Chickasaws, 1971)

In 1818, the United States government conducted a Chickasaw census as a part of their various schemes to gradually force the southern tribes westward. Prior to this, President Jefferson had aided this objective by implementing a strategy of debt from which the Chickasaws would only be able to repay through the sale of their lands. When indebtedness of the tribe reached the saturation point, the United States swiftly implemented treaty negotiations with the Chickasaw Tribe, which aggressively included the ceding of tribal lands. Although opposition from the Chickasaws was fierce, the treaties of the 1830s became inevitable, and among other sacrifices, provided for all the southeastern tribes to cede portions of their land in southern Kentucky, Tennessee, Alabama and Mississippi.

Meanwhile, missionaries, mission educators and well-meaning southerners established schools and churches among the tribes. While moving westward, the colonists were constantly reminded that this land had been the home to many tribes. Although these native people bitterly opposed the colonists' westward migration, expansion continued. In 1832, after much heated negotiation with the United States, the Chickasaws agreed to move only if tribal officials and other appointed members were able to locate a suitable area for their new home.

Chickasaw Chief Piomingo, Levi Colbert and other tribal leaders negotiated conditions concerning the Chickasaw removal during numerous meetings with the United States in Washington, D.C. Levi Colbert led three trips to Indian Territory (now Oklahoma) to search for suitable land. After these trips, he was still not satisfied with any of the land he had seen. Unfortunately, Levi passed away in the middle of these negotiations from a prolonged illness. By this time, Edmund Pickens had become active in the tribe and was involved in these negotiations. It was a very difficult time for the Chickasaw people. Levi Colbert's death caused further anxiety. Unfortunately, the United States would not be denied that land. Under the new leadership of George Colbert, Levi's brother, Chickasaws continued to negotiate for a favorable removal treaty. Eventually both parties arrived at an agreement and the Chickasaw people were forced to move west, whether they had found a suitable home or not.

In Mississippi, families had adequate land and good hunting. Members had been attending church regularly at the Monroe Mission and the children had been able to attend school. Their territory and their way of life were perfect in the eyes of the Chickasaws. To leave was heartbreaking.

FAREWELL TO MONROE MISSION

C H A P T E R   F O U R

One can only imagine the anguish the Chickasaw people felt as they embarked on this new chapter of their lives. As they prepared to leave the land of their ancestors, heading toward an uncertain future, sadness, fear and worry must have gripped them. However, the Chickasaw people are a proud and resourceful tribe. I believe they would have remained positive and tried to make the best out of their difficult situation. The following prose is what the author feels might have happened during the final service of Monroe Mission:

"No autumn day in history could possibly surpass this one," said Father Thomas C. Stuart, as he closed his Bible and looked at the congregation of the crowded Monroe Mission. The electric silence in the recently enlarged log structure seemed to forecast the explosion of emotions among the mission's members. Never before had every member of Monroe Mission been present for so momentous an occasion – the final service prior to the departure of the Chickasaw tribe for their new home west of the Mississippi.

Monroe Mission by Ann Sheffield.
[Image courtesy of the Chickasaw Nation Art Collection]

"My enormous mission family," mused Father Stuart as he looked out on a congregation that consisted of many cultures and races. The missionary caught his breath as he saw Edmund Pickens (Okchantubby) slowly rise to his feet and, in a clear, baritone voice, begin to sing a capella in his native tongue. He was singing that old hymn, *Amazing Grace*, brought by Father Stuart 16 years before from the Presbyterian Synod of South Carolina. By impulse, Father Stuart joined Edmund in song, along with their friend, Benjamin Love. Then, the entire congregation rose to their feet and completed the unique harmony of Chickasaws in divine worship. The voices ranged from the Chickasaws themselves, to the southern dialect of intermarried spouses and friends, to the slaves and the few Creek and Cherokee Indians who were present. The mixture of English and Chickasaw words struck Father

Stuart. For a split second, it sounded like what he imagined had taken place long ago on Pentecost – when the Holy Spirit appeared to the disciples after Easter.

Everyone raised their voices in song, perhaps sensing that they would never have the opportunity to do so again. With the windows open, the overflow crowd that had assembled under the arbor joined in as well. The whole countryside seemed to reverberate with reverent but tragic pathos of this unique experience.

They all remained on their feet at the end of the last verse. Many leaned heavily on the handmade pews, reluctant to break the spell.

"This," said Father Stuart, "is the last service in Monroe Mission before you depart for your new home in the west. A service like this will never take place again, but believe me – it will remain in our hearts and memories forever! The good Lord, through the Presbyterian Synod of South Carolina, led me to you, my dear friends. Counted among my dear friends, were Brother David Pickens, our co-worker and fellow mis-sionary who managed the farm for several years, and who now rests in our little cemetery across the road. There were many other co-workers: our friend, Reverend Cyrus Byington, who visited us in our homes and baptized many of you; James Vernon, our mechanic; and our special assistant, Joseph Adams – each one of us had a place in our congregation. The more we learned together, the more we began to love and respect each other.

My hope is that your children will take these lessons with them. Our God brought us together here and at Martyn, our joint mission, and other places too. He will remain with us as we assume a new phase of our existence. My family has been your family. So now, may God be with us forevermore." Choking with emotion, Father Stuart's voice trailed off into the hymn, *God Be With You 'Till We Meet Again.* The whole congregation soon joined in. Thus, a final farewell hymn closed the service. The members stood in profound silence as if frozen, loathe to leave the sanctuary.

The cry of a child cut into the stillness of that warm September day, then another muffled moan. The middle-aged stoical Molly Gunn stifled a sob, determined to leave the mission in her familiar pleasant manner, regardless of the circumstances. Her deceased husband, old Scottish highlander James Gunn, had been one of the first to become a member of Monroe Mission on December 4, 1824. Then Colonel James Colbert stepped to the front. His raised voice boomed out, the Scottish brogue slightly noticeable.

"Friends and relatives, we've said goodbye before, but always within this, our Chickasaw Nation. We're leaving behind hundreds of years of memories. We recall well the circumstances when this mission was established. How my brother, William Colbert, donated the land for the mission and for Father Stuart's home not far from here. Now, we leave him and our deceased families. Our grandfathers of past generations are asleep in the warm earth on which we have always lived. Yes, we must leave our sacred ground that was given to us by God. But we are a strong and determined people, and if we stand united, we will leave this place with courage. We will make a good life for ourselves, our children and our grandchildren, despite this disruption of our lives."

James, the educated son of James Logan Colbert, was one of the earliest traders from Scotland to marry into the Chickasaw tribe. He continued, "Remember, we still have each other and this is only a sad step into the future. Soon we will begin our journey. Many will gather at Pontitock and other places. Then we will go to the Chickasaw Bluffs and depart together for our new home. My late brother Levi (Itawamba Minko), who now sleeps at Buzzard Roost, and those who made the journey with him, found a new home for us. They climbed over the strong, green mountains and drank from the clear, sparkling springs. The tall, green grass of the meadows will be good food for our livestock. They saw the sun rise and set over the tall pines and oaks of the forest – just like the sacred land we are now leaving. Our animal brothers are plentiful; there will be enough food for us all. Our fellow Chickasaws who found the land have dealt with our Choctaw brothers and made a treaty with them. When we leave this land along the ridge, the Tombigbee River, Pontitock Creek and our sacred homes, we will be going to another suitable place to establish homes for our families and future generations. Now, may our God be with us all as we bid farewell to Father Stuart and his family and to all our missionary friends. Yakkookay!" he proclaimed, which means "thank you."

The eloquent Chickasaw leader turned, and with calm, confident dignity, strode down the aisle, portraying all the strength for which he was known. Young Cyrus Harris, who had served as an interpreter and special assistant in many of the land reserve assignments involved in the Treaty of May 24, 1834, turned to follow his great-uncle, impressed and deeply moved by his speech. Following next were Cyrus' stepfather and mother, Malcom and Elizabeth Oxberry McGee, his grandmother, Molly Gunn, and his aunt, Rhoda Gunn Potts. They were followed by Cyrus' half-sister, Jane McGee and her husband, William R. Guy.

Family after family left the crowded mission. Edmund Pickens and his wife, Liney and their children, Rachel, Mary, David and Johnson; the Kemp brothers – Jackson and Joel and their families, along with their siblings and families; Bernard McLaughlin, stepfather of Edmund Pickens, and the entire family of McLaughlins; the John Bynums; Henry and Sarah Love and their children; James Boyd and family; James Allen and his family; Kunnoeyi; Mrs. William Colbert; the James Perry family; William H. Barr and his family; Charlotte James; Mrs. Mary Gunn and many others. Father Stuart greeted each one as they slowly left the mission, making a remark to each. All the others outside were mingling with friends and relatives. Father Stuart surveyed the overflow crowd. He saw the James McLish family and Aaron Brown, who was with his family and cousins. James Holmes, who had come to them from Carlyle, Pennsylvania and was a ruling elder in this church, was also outside greeting the congregation as they departed. Some of the black members included Prince, Sokey, Bekky, Miney, Nellie, Leah, and Sophia; also Samuel Pearson and his family, and Mrs. Colbert. Other black members who had united with the church were Manuel, Reuben, Jennet and Chrissy.

Father Stuart spoke to Thomas and Elizabeth Cheadle, Sally Fraser, Nuseka and Dicey Colbert, Tuppeha, Ishtimayi, Tushkaiahokti, Pohaiki, Polly Hogan, Walton James, the Blairs and their children, Betsy, a Creek woman plus many others who were preparing to leave. Each would remain in the memory of Father Stuart. Thoughts of each member's baptism flashed through Father Stuart's mind. Soon, the little mission was quiet except for the diminishing commotion on the outside as carriage after carriage left the grounds. Father Stuart walked into the front yard.

He saw several young children lingering about. There were tears on the tan cheeks of a girl who was old enough to grasp the seriousness of the situation. She clutched a New Testament Father Stuart had presented to her for a perfect attendance record. Another child carried a shuck doll made from cornhusks. Her parents had allowed her to bring it to church that morning. The lined faces of two of the last elderly women to leave the grounds were red from weeping. Young and old alike seemed to share a slightly puzzled appearance – the sadness of temporary separation from their friends and relatives, and the permanent departure from Monroe Mission with all its memories. Muffled sobs were beginning to change to excited chattering. Children who had known each other since infancy held hands as their gait changed from walking, to skipping, then to jumping and running. Edmund Pickens turned to his wife Liney. She lifted her head proudly, determined to show her children that all was well. Whether they wanted to or not, they had to make a new home. No need to excite the children any more than they already were, she thought.

Liney thought to herself, could it be that she and the three older children had been baptized *six* years ago? May 1, 1831 had been such a beautiful day. That day they were all baptized, except Johnson, who had been visiting his cousin. Johnson was baptized later that year, on September 11. Edmund had been baptized a year earlier. Liney thought back to April 1, 1830, when Edmund had talked with Reverend Cyrus Byington about joining the church. Also present that day were Sally Fraser, Nuseka and Dicey Colbert, Betsy (the Creek woman), along with a black woman named Amy Syke.

Reverend Byington was a well-known missionary who had spent years with the Choctaw people. Reverend Byington visited Father Stuart and other missionaries whenever possible and often baptized new members. Going back even further, Edmund's stepfather, Bernard McLaughlin, who was admitted to the church on December 4, 1824, had been influential in bringing the entire family into the congregation.

Edmund slowly helped each child into the carriage, then drove approximately one hundred yards and stopped. "We simply must wait for the Stuarts," he said. "Of all days, we cannot allow them to travel home alone. Let's drive along with them for a couple of miles."

He handed the reins to Liney. Stepping down from the carriage, he walked the short distance back to the sanctuary as his family watched. The children chatted quietly as Liney drove the carriage into the shade of a large oak tree. Liney sat, thinking about the plans for the day. They would go to her father-in-law's home to assist Bernard and Edmund's sisters and brothers in preparing for the long journey westward. Then they would go to the little cemetery plot near the house, where their relatives were buried.

Liney recalled Edmund telling her about the death of his father, John Pickens, at Natchez on January 18, 1789, before Edmund was born. She thought about the will, the probate of John's estate, his mother returning to the Chickasaw Nation and Edmund's early years. Liney sighed. After the noon meal with the McLaughlins, they would proceed home, probably stopping to spend the night with friends. Then they would leave early for home, past Susan Guest's home, possibly stopping for at moment to see the Thomas family and Betsy. There might also be a few of their cousins to visit briefly.

Liney visualized the new wagons Edmund had recently bought. Freshly painted and sturdy, they should make the trip to Indian Territory in good condition. Edmund had purchased necessary supplies from the trading post at the bluffs several days before. Unlike some of his relatives, his trading was done at the little town of Somerville, which was north in the state of Tennessee, and Holly Springs, which was several miles from their home on the Tennessee line. They had prepared very carefully for the long journey, and they were determined to bring everything they owned with them. When they arrived home, Edmond and the boys would round up the livestock. Edmund had conveyed their property by three deeds, so most of the Pickens land in the old Chickasaw Nation had been worked diligently. Liney sighed again. In a few moments, they would be on their way, leaving all these places behind. Soon, all this would only exist as memories.

Edmund found Father Stuart, his wife Susan, and their daughter Mary Jane still inside the mission. Grasping Father Stuart's hand, Edmund looked straight into the eyes of the missionary, his own blue-eyed gaze held that of his kindly, beloved pastor and friend for a long moment. Then, the firm, strong handshake melted into a quick hug and Father Stuart said in the kindly voice so familiar to Edmund, "God be with you 'till we meet again, Edmund!" With a final hug from each

of the women, Edmund turned and strode down the steps
to the grass, then started walking down the road to his own
waiting carriage.

The usual lunch on the grounds that day was cancelled; food
would be awaiting the arrival of everyone at home, for this was
a very special day. Many of the members had gone to the little
cemetery across the road to bid farewell to those who had been
laid to rest there. As though trying to imprint the inscriptions
on the headstones into their memories forever, they stared in
silence; others knelt briefly in prayer. One small child, who
was there with his mother, stood hugging the headstone of
his recently departed father. A young orphan boy attempted
to bury fieldstones at the graves of his parents. The freshly
mounded soil appeared to be only days old. After all, diseases
brought into the Chickasaw Nation by their white neighbors
had taken their toll. With no immunity to plagues such as
smallpox, this young couple, like many others, had fallen prey.
How the young child was spared had been a mystery to his
aunt and uncle, who were now taking his hand and leading
him to their buggy. The uncle turned suddenly, returned to
the graves and made sure the stones were firmly in place. He
would rear his brother and sister-in-law's son as best he could.
With a slight salute, he whispered, "I promise ..." returned to
his wife and nephew, and then drove away.

By this time, carriages of all sorts – buggies, surreys, wagons
and many horseback riders – were disappearing around the
curves to the east, south and west. Families were anxious to
return home. Most went northward toward Pontotoc, where
they had been camped for the last few days, awaiting final
orders to leave for the west. Excited conversations mingled

with softly sung hymns. Some shouts could be heard from the distance before finally, all was quiet.

Father Stuart and his family checked the outside buildings, which had been used for cooking and dining for the past 14 years, and closed all the windows. Then he returned to the sanctuary. Father Stuart touched each pew as he went down the aisle to pick up his well-worn Bible from the pulpit. All holding hands, the Stuart family knelt in one last prayer of thanksgiving. They prayed for the work of the missionaries, for their friends and for the safety and happiness of all as they came to this crossroad of life. There were so many fond memories. There were difficulties, joys and sorrows, and tragedies and triumphs. Most of all, they felt privileged to know all these friends whom some in the South Carolina Synod had referred to as "heathens." Imagine that, he thought, with a slight feeling of disgust. I just wish they could see all these good people now. Heathens, indeed!

The many baptisms went through his mind. Entire families were now Christian, whether they were Indian, white or black. True, some had never professed Christianity, but many others had been on the verge when the land cession negotiations began. Unfortunately, these diversionary events had interrupted their work.

Father Stuart himself had buried several friends, and although he would not be leaving this mission, it would never be the same without "his Chickasaws." Surely he would visit these Chickasaw friends when they were settled in their new homes. It was the recently deceased "old General," William Colbert, who had given them the land on which to build the mission and the parsonage (approximately two miles from the mission). Like many others, Father Stuart had helped William through difficult times. George, younger brother of William Colbert, had become very cordial with Father Stuart too. Yes, Father Stuart was grateful to the Lord for entrusting so many Chickasaw friends to him for safekeeping. Incidents too numerous to mention flashed through his mind at that sacred moment.

Father Stuart wiped away a tear and closed his prayer. He locked the front door and gave it a slight pat, as if touching the shoulder of an old friend. Then he, Susan and Mary Jane went quietly down to the waiting carriage. Abraham, who had been the slave of General and Mrs. Colbert, waited to assist them into the buggy. Abraham's wife Eliza and their children were there too. Abraham handed the reins to Father Stuart. A 13-year member of Monroe Mission, this gesture was not new to Abraham. This duty – attending to Father Stuart's buggy and horse – had been assigned to him by the General following the baptism of several members of his family.

Father Stuart recalled how the Chickasaws had come to the mission with their slaves and encouraged them to join the church. Abraham had been born to one of the Colbert slaves and was among the first to join. He had grown up at Tockshish, a few miles south of Monroe Mission, and Abraham felt his roots were there. So, this honor meant much to him. He had looked forward to assisting Father Stuart, an outstanding man in his opinion, for several years.

Father Stuart, Susan and Mary Jane each hugged the members of Abraham's family. With a long glance back at the mission, the Stuarts stepped into the buggy. Since October 1831, the mission had been under the Presbytery of Tombeckbee, and Father Stuart would soon be back at the mission. Unfortunately, it would be without his beloved Chickasaws and the other members who had attended the service that day.

Although the Stuarts' buggy had been under the same large shade tree at the back of the church, it seemed a little warm now, and they were anxious to start toward home. They found the Pickens carriage at the bend of the road in the shade. Edmund's family called out a final farewell to their friends, waited for the Stuarts to go on ahead, and then both proceeded on their way home.

Now, excitement seemed to fill the air. Liney again thought about the meal for the large family. Their daughter Cassandra had stayed home today to prepare the noon meal. She had promised a traditional Chickasaw menu of pashofa, grape dumplings and fry bread. What a good cook Cassandra was, mused Liney. Presently, all was quiet again.

For miles, the only sound was the clip-clop of horses on the hard, dirt road. Edmund's eyes again took on a look of sadness as he drove down this ancient road. He could not remember a time when he had *not* traveled the road. He believed he knew each tree, each bush, each cluster of sumac; the wild grape vines and wild plums; as well as each rock along the road. Looking longingly at the cornfields, he also noticed a field of cotton. It simply did not seem right that the fields weren't filled with people picking those crops. (When the Chickasaws sold their land, they were obliged to include the ripening crops in their sale.) In all likelihood, this would be the last time Edmund's family would travel this road. Sadly, he thought, it seemed to him that they had been living in what Father Stuart had described as the Garden of Eden.

Waiting in line to claim their reserves with Edmund were hundreds of other men and women, including close friends and relatives. Many complete families were there, but some family members chose to be absent on this emotional but historic occasion. After a busy day, Edmund and his family started the long trek home, observing every beautiful foot of the area. After all, they had grown up here. They had played along the path, climbed the trees, fished in nearby streams and hunted in the area. They had tended the cattle and horses, assisted with the butchering of animals and performed many other chores. Along the way, they were greeted by friends and relatives who lingered to discuss the upcoming journey.

The following months passed quickly for the families. The preparations needed for the move to their new home were extensive. They had to purchase new clothes for the entire family, new wagons, a sturdy buggy and all kinds of equipment. The Chickasaws had long since occupied good modern homes, but they would have to rebuild. Besides their homes, there were many other items they would have to leave behind. Even though they were burdened with many thoughts, most families, including the Pickens, Colberts, Kemps, Keels and other relatives of Edmund Pickens went about the usual lifestyle of "intelligent acceptance."

"Soon we begin our journey. We all know that many will gather at Pontitock, and then go to Chickasaw Bluffs, and we will depart in groups for the new home we have been told about. Believe me, my brother Itawamba Minko, Levi, and the others we sent, saw it. The walked over the strong, green mountain; they drank from the clear, sparkling streams and the green grass of the meadows rose up to welcome them. They saw the sun rise and set above the tall pines of the forests. Our animal brothers are abundant and our feathered friends send a welcome to them. They conferred and dealt with our Choctaw brothers in the land where we are going. As they told us, it will not be this land along the ridge that we all love, but it will be a friendly, abundant home for us. Now, may Pinki' Chihoowa be with us all forevermore."

The rugged old Chickasaw leader of the House of Incus-she-wa-yah turned, and with calm, confident dignity strode down the aisle, depicting all the strength for which he was known. Young Cyrus Harris, wont to follow his great-uncle, took the arm of his mother, Elizabeth McGee, and then released it to his stepfather, Malcolm McGee. Reaching for the arm of his aunt Rhoda Gunn who, with only a year's difference in their ages, had grown up with her nephew, together they followed their parents, along with Cyrus' half-sister, Jane.

Family after family left the little mission – the Kemp brothers, Jackson and Joel and their families; Major James Colbert, half-brother of George, Levi and General William, his family with him, bade friends and relatives a temporary goodbye. Then Bynums, Boyds, Loves and Allens were seen mingling with relatives and friends. James McLish and Aaron Brown started for the door, followed by the Holmes family, the Moores, Fraziers, and others. Soon the litte mission was silent.

Thus ends this author's narrative on the last few days at Monroe Mission and in the surrounding Chickasaw territory. Based on their faith and their strength of character, Edmund, his family and all the other Chickasaws were equal to the challenge that lay ahead of them.

THE REMOVAL

C H A P T E R   F I V E

In the midst of the greatest mass exodus of a people since the inception of the United States of America, the Chickasaw Tribe, along with many others, suffered untold hardship because of their treaties with the Unites States. The Great Removal of the Chickasaw people was in accordance with the 1832 Treaty of Pontitock.

TREATY WITH THE CHICKASAW (1832, Oct. 20)

7 Stat. 381.
Proclamation March 1, 1833.

Articles of a treaty made and entered into between Genl. John Coffee, being duly authorised thereto, by the President of the United States, and the whole Chickasaw Nation, in General Council assembled, at the Council House, on Pontitock Creek on the twentieth day of October, 1832.

THE Chickasaw Nation find themselves oppressed in their present situation; by being made subject to the laws of the States in which they reside. Being ignorant of

the language and laws of the white man, they cannot understand or obey them. Rather than submit to this great evil, they
prefer to seek a home in the west, where they may live and be
governed by their own laws. And believing that they can procure for themselves a home, in a country suited to their wants
and condition, provided they had the means to contract and
pay for the same, they have determined to sell their country
and hunt a new home. The President has heard the complaints
of the Chickasaws, and like them believes they cannot be
happy, and prosper as a nation, in their present situation and
condition, and being desirous to relieve them from the great ca-
lamity that seems to await them, if they remain as they are. He
has sent his Commissioner Genl. John Coffee, who has met the
whole Chickasaw nation in Council, and after mature delibera-
tion, they have entered into the following articles, which shall
be binding on both parties, when the same shall be ratified by
the President of the United States by and with the advice and
consent of the Senate.

ARTICLE 1. For the consideration hereinafter expressed, the
Chickasaw nation do hereby cede, to the United States, all the
land which they own on the east side of the Mississippi river,
including all the country where they at present live and occupy.

ARTICLE 2. The United States agree to have the whole country thus ceded, surveyed, as soon as it can be conveniently
done, in the same manner that the public lands of the United
States are surveyed in the States of Mississippi and Alabama,
and as soon thereafter as may be practicable, to have the same
prepared for sale. The President of the United States will then
offer the land for sale at public auction, in the same manner and on the same terms and conditions as the other public

lands, and such of the land as may not sell at the public sales shall be offered at private sale, in the same manner that other private sales are made of the United States lands.

ARTICLE 3. As a full compensation to the Chickasaw nation, for the country thus ceded, the United States agree to pay over to the Chickasaw nation, all the money arising from the sale of the land which may be received from time to time, after deducting therefrom the whole cost and expenses of surveying and selling the land, including every expense attending the same.

ARTICLE 4. The President being determined that the Chickasaw people shall not deprive themselves of a comfortable home, in the country where they now are, until they shall have provided a country in the west to remove to, and settle on, with fair prospects of future comfort and happiness, It is therefore agreed to, by the Chickasaw nation, that they will endeavor as soon as it may be in their power, after the ratification of this treaty, to hunt out and procure a home for their people, west of the Mississippi river, suited to their wants and condition; and they will continue to do so during the progress of the survey of their present country, as is provided for in the second article of this treaty. But should they fail to procure such a country to remove to and settle on, previous to the first public sale of their country here then and in that event, they are to select out of the surveys, a comfortable settlement for every family in the Chickasaw nation, to include their present improvements, if the land is good for cultivation, and if not they may take it in any other place in the nation, which is unoccupied by any other person. Such settlement must be taken by sections. And there shall be allotted to each family as follows (to wit): To a single man who is twenty-one years of age, one section to each family of five and under that number two sections to each family of six and not exceeding ten, three sections, and to each family over ten in number, four sections and to families who own slaves, there shall be allowed, one section to those who own ten or upwards and such as own under ten, there shall be allowed half a section. If any person shall now occupy two places and wish to retain both, they may do so, by taking a part at one place, and a part at the other, and where two or more persons are now living on the same section, the oldest occupant will be entitled to remain, and the others must move off to some other place if so required by the oldest occupant. All of which tracts of land so selected and retained, shall be held, and occupied by the Chickasaw people, uninterrupted until they shall find and obtain a country suited to their wants and condition. And the United States will guaranty to the Chickasaw nation, the quiet possession and uninterrupted use of the said reserved tracts of land, so long as they may live on and occupy the same. And when they shall determine to remove from said tracts of land, the Chickasaw nation will notify the President of the United States of their determination to remove, and thereupon as soon as the Chickasaw people shall remove, the President will proclaim the said reserved tracts of land for sale at public auction and at private sale, on the same terms and conditions, as is provided for in the second article of this treaty, to sell the same, and the net proceeds thereof, to be paid to the Chickasaw nation, as is provided for in the third article of this treaty.

ARTICLE 5. If any of the Chickasaw families shall have made valuable improvements on the places where they lived and removed from, on the reservation tracts, the same shall be valued by some discreet person to be appointed by the President, who shall assess the real cash value of all such improvements, and

also the real cash value of all the land within their improvements, which they may have cleared and actually cultivated, at
least one year in good farming order and condition. And such
valuation of the improvements and the value of the cultivated
lands as before mentioned, shall be paid to the person who
shall have made the same. To be paid out of the proceeds of
the sales of the ceded lands. The person who shall value such
land and improvements, shall give to the owner thereof, a
certificate of the valuation, which shall be a good voucher for
them to draw the money on, from the proper person, who shall
be appointed to pay the same, and the money shall be paid, as
soon as may be convenient, after the valuation, to enable the
owner thereof to provide for their families on their journey to
their new homes. The provisions of this article are intended to
encourage industry and to enable the Chickasaws to move comfortably. But least the good intended may be abused, by design-
ing persons, by hiring hands and clearing more land, than they
otherwise would do for the benefit of their families. It is determined that no payment shall be made for improved lands, over
and above one-eighth part of the tract allowed and reserved for
such person to live on and occupy.

ARTICLE 6. The Chickasaw nation cannot receive any part
of the payment for their land until it shall be surveyed and
sold; therefore, in order to the greater facilitate, in surveying
and preparing the land for sale, and for keeping the business
of the nation separate and apart from the business and ac-
counts of the United States, it is proposed by the Chickasaws,
and agreed to, that a Surveyor General be appointed by the
President, by and with the advice and consent of the Senate,
to superintend alone the surveying of this ceded country or so
much thereof as the President may direct, who shall appoint a

sufficient number of deputy surveyors, as may be necessary to complete the survey, in as short a time as may be reasonable and expedient. That the said Surveyor General be allowed one good clerk, and one good draftsman to aid and assist him in the business of his office, in preparing the lands for sale. It is also agreed that one land office be established for the sale of the lands, to have one Register and one Receiver of monies, to be appointed by the President, by and with the advice and consent of the Senate, and each Register and Receiver to have one good clerk to aid and assist them in the duties of their office. The Surveyor's office, and the office of the Register and Receiver of money, shall be kept somewhere central in the nation, at such place as the President of the United States may direct. As the before mentioned officers, and clerks, are to be employed entirely in business of the nation, appertaining to preparing and selling the land, they will of course be paid out of the proceeds of the sales of the ceded lands. That the Chickasaws, may now understand as near as may be, the expenses that will be incurred in the transacting of this business. It is proposed and agreed to, that the salary of the Surveyor General be fifteen hundred dollars a year, and that the Register and Receiver of monies, be allowed twelve hundred dollars a year each, as a full compensation for their services, and all expenses, except stationary and postages on their official business, and that each of the clerks and draftsman be allowed seven hundred and fifty dollars a year, for their services and all expenses.

ARTICLE 7. It is expressly agreed that the United States shall not grant any right of preference, to any person, or right of occupancy in any manner whatsoever, but in all cases, of either public or private sale, they are to sell the land to the highest bidder, and also that none of the lands be sold in smaller tracts than quarter sections or fractional sections of the same size as near as may be, until the Chickasaw nation may require the President to sell in smaller tracts. The Chiefs of the nation have heard that at some of the sales of the United States lands, the people there present, entered into combinations, and united in purchasing much of the land, at reduced prices, for their own benefit, to the great prejudice of the Government, and they express fears, that attempts will be made to cheat them, in the same manner when their lands shall be offered at public auction. It is therefore agreed that the President will use his best endeavours to prevent such combinations, or any other plan or state of things which may tend to prevent the land selling for its full value.

ARTICLE 8. As the Chickasaws have determined to sell their country, it is desirable that the nation realize the great-est possible sum for their lands, which can be obtained. It is therefore proposed and agreed to that after the President shall have offered their lands for sale and shall have sold all that will sell for the Government price, then the price shall be reduced, so as to induce purchasers to buy, who would not take the land at the Government minimum price; and it is believed, that five years from and after the date of the first sale, will dispose of all the lands, that will sell at the Govern-ment price. If then at the expiration of five years, as before mentioned, the Chickasaw nation may request the President to sell at such reduced price as the nation may then propose, it shall be the duty of the President to comply with their request, by first offering it at public and afterwards at private sale, as in all other cases of selling public lands.

ARTICLE 9. The Chickasaw nation express their ignorance, and incapacity to live, and be happy under the State laws, they cannot read and understand them, and therefore they will always need a friend to advise and direct them. And fearing at some day the Government of the United States may withdraw from them, the agent under whose instructions they have lived so long and happy, they therefore request that the agent may be continued with them, while here, and wherever they may remove to and settle. It is the earnest wish of the United States Government to see the Chickasaw nation prosper and be happy, and so far as is consistent they will contribute all in their power to render them so therefore their request is granted. There shall be an agent kept with the Chickasaws as heretofore, so long as they live within the jurisdiction of the United States as a nation, either within the limits of the States where they now reside, or at any other place. And whenever the office of agent shall be vacant, and an agent to be appointed, the President will pay due respect to the wishes of the nation in selecting a man in all respects qualified to discharge the responsible duties of that office.

ARTICLE 10. Whenever the Chickasaw nation shall determine to remove from, and leave their present country, they will give the President of the United States timely notice of such intention, and the President will furnish them, the necessary funds, and means for their transportation and journey, and for one years provisions, after they reach their new homes, in such quantity as the nation may require, and the full amount of such funds, transportation and provisions, is to be paid for, out of the proceeds of the sales of the ceded lands. And should the Chickasaw nation remove, from their present country, before they receive money, from the sale of the lands, hereby ceded; then and in that case, the United States shall furnish them any reasonable stun of money for national purposes, which may be deemed proper by the President of the United States, which sum shall also be refunded out of the sales of the ceded lands.

ARTICLE 11. The Chickasaw nation have determined to create a perpetual fund, for the use of the nation forever, out of the proceeds of the country now ceded away. And for that purpose they propose to invest a large proportion of the money arising from the sale of the land, in some safe and valuable stocks, which will bring them in an annual interest or dividend, to be used for all national purposes, leaving the principal untouched, intending to use the interest alone. It is therefore proposed by the Chickasaws, and agreed to, that the sum to be laid out in stocks as above mentioned, shall be left with the government of the United States, until it can be laid out under the direction of the President of the United States, by and with the advice and consent of the Senate, in such safe and valuable stock as he may approve of, for the use and benefit of the Chickasaw nation. The sum thus to be invested, shall be equal to, at least three-fourths of the whole net proceeds of the sales of the lands; and as much more, as the nation may determine, if there shall be a surplus after sup-plying all the national wants. But it is hereby provided, that if the reasonable wants of the nation shall require more than one fourth Of the proceeds of the sales of the land, then they may, by the consent of the President and Senate, draw from the government such sum as may be thought reasonable, for valuable national purposes, out of the three-fourths reserved to be laid out in stocks. But if any of the monies shall be thus drawn out of the sum first proposed, to be laid out on interest, the stall shall be replaced, out of the first monies of the nation, which may come into the possession of the United States government, from the sale of the ceded lands, over and above the reasonable wants of the nation. At the expiration of fifty years from this date, if the Chickasaw nation shall have improved in education and civilization, and become so enlightened, as to be capable of managing so large a sum of money to advantage, and with safety, for the benefit of the nation, and the President of the United States, with the Senate, shall be satisfied thereof, at that time, and shall give their consent thereto, the Chickasaw nation may then withdraw the whole, or any part of the fund now set apart, to be laid out in stocks, or at interest, and dispose of the same, in any manner that they may think proper at that time, for the use and benefit of the whole nation; but no part of said fund shall ever be used for any other purpose, than the benefit of the whole Chickasaw nation. In order to facilitate the survey and sale of the lands now ceded, and to raise the money therefrom as soon as possible, for the foregoing purpose, the President of the United States is authorised to commence the survey of the land as soon as may be practicable, after the ratification of this treaty.

ARTICLE 12. The Chickasaws feel grateful to their old chiefs, for their long and faithful services, in attending to the business of the nation. They believe it a duty, to keep them from want in their old and declining age with those feelings, they have looked upon their old and beloved chief Tish-o-mingo, who is now grown old, and is poor and not able to live, in that comfort, which his valuable life and great merit deserve. It is therefore determined to give him out of the national funds, one hundred dollars a year during the balance of his life, and the nation request him to receive it, as a token of their kind feelings for him, on account of his long and valuable services.

Our old and beloved Queen Pue-caunda, is now very old and very poor. Justice says the nation ought not to let her suffer in her old age; it is therefore determined to give her out of the national funds, fifty dollars a year during her life, the money to be put in the hands of the agent to be laid out for her support, under his direction, with the advice of the chiefs.

ARTICLE 13. The boundary line between the lands of the Chickasaws and Choctaws, has never been run, or properly defined, and as the Choctaws have sold their country to the United States, they now have no interest in the decision of that question. It is therefore agreed to call on the old Choctaw chiefs to determine the line to be run, between the Chickasaws and their former country. The Chickasaws, by a treaty made with the United States at Franklin in Tennessee, in Aug. 31, 1830, (a) declared their line to run as follows, to wit: Beginning at the mouth of Oak tibby-haw and running up said stream to a point, being a marked tree, on the old Natches road, one mile south-wardly from Wall's old place. Thence with the Choctaw bound-ary, and along it, westwardly through the Tunicha old fields, to a point on the Mississippi river, about twenty-eight miles by water, below where the St. Francis river enter said stream on the west side. It is now agreed, that the surveys of the Choc-taw country which are now in progress, shall not cross the line until the true line shall be decided and determined; which shall be done as follows, the agent of the (Choctaws on the west side of the Mississippi shall call on the old and intelligent chiefs of that nation, and lay before them the line as claimed by the Chickasaws at the Franklin treaty, and if the Choctaws shall determine that line to be correct, then it shall be established and made the permanent line, but if the Choctaws say the line strikes the Mississippi river higher up said stream, then the best evidence which can be had from both nations, shall be taken by the agents of both nations, and submitted to the President of the United States for his decision, and on such evidence, the President will determine the true line on principles of strict justice.

ARTICLE 14. As soon as the surveys are made, it shall be the duty of the chiefs, with the advice and assistance of the agent to cause a correct list to be made out of all and every tract of land, which shall be reserved, for the use and benefit of the Chickasaw people, for their residence, as is provided for in the fourth article of this treaty, which list, will designate the sections of land, which are set apart for each family or individual in the nation, shewing the precise tracts which shall belong to each and every one of them, which list shall be returned to the register of the land office, and he shall make a record of the same, in his office, to prevent him from offering any of said tracts of land for sale, and also as evidence of each person's lands. All the residue of the lands will be offered by the President for sale.

The Chickasaws request that no persons be permitted to move in and settle on their country before the land is sold. It is therefore agreed, that no person, whatsoever, who is not Chickasaw or connected with the Chickasaws by marriage, shall be permitted to come into the country and settle on any part of the ceded lands until they shall be offered for sale, and then there shall not be any person permitted to settle on any of the land, which has not been sold, at the time of such settlement, and in all cases of a person settling on any of the ceded lands contrary to this express understanding, they will be intruders, and must be treated as such, and put off of the lands of the nation.

In witness of all and every thing herein determined, between the United States and the whole Chickasaw nation in general council assembled, the parties have hereunto set their hands and seals, at the council-house, on Pontitock creek, in the Chickasaw nation, on the twentieth day of October, one thousand eight hundred and thirty-two.

John Coffee,

Ish-te-ho-to-pa, (king) his x mark,
Tish-o-min-go, his x mark,
Levi Colbert, his x mark,
George Colbert, his x mark,
William M'Gilvery, his x mark,
Samuel Sely, his x mark,
To-pul-kah, his x mark,
Isaac Albertson, his x mark,
Em-ub-by, his x mark,
Pis-tah-lah-tubbe, his x mark,
Ish-tim-o-lut-ka, his x mark,
James Brown, his x mark,
Im-mah-hoo-lo-tubbe, his x mark,
Ish-ta-ha-chah, his x mark,
Lah-fin-hubbe, his x mark,
Shop-pow-me, his x mark,
Nin-uck-ah-umba, his x mark,
lm-mah-hoo-la-tubbe, his x mark,

Illup-pah-umba, his x mark,

Pitman Colbert,

Con-mush-ka-ish-kah, his x mark,

James Wolfe,

Bah-ha-kah-tubbe, his x mark,

E. Bah-kah-tubbe, his x mark,

Captain Thompson, his x mark,

New-berry, his x mark,

Bah-ma-hah-tubbe, his x mark,

John Lewis, his x mark,

I-yah-hou-tubbe, his x mark,

Tok-holth-la-chah, his x mark,

Oke-lah-nah-nubbe, his x mark,

Im-me-tubbe, his x mark,

In-kah-yea, his x mark,

Ah-sha-eubbe, his x mark,

Im-mah-ho-bah, his x mark,

Fit-ehah-pla, his x mark,

Unte-mi-ah-tubbe, his x mark,

Oke-lah-hin-lubbe, his x mark,

John Glover, his x mark,

Bah-me-hubbe, his x mark,

Hush-tah-tah-ubbe, his x mark,

Un-ti-ha-kah-tubbe, his x mark,

Yum-mo-tubbe, his x mark,

Oh-ha-cubbe, his x mark,

Ah-fab-mah, his x mark,

Ah-ta-kin-tubbe, his x mark,

Ah-to-ko-wah, his x mark,

Tah-ha-cubbe, his x mark,

Kin-hoi-cha, his x mark,

Ish-te-ah-tubbe, his x mark,

Chick-ah-shah-nan-ubbe, his x mark,

Che-wut-ta-ha, his x mark,

Fo-lut-ta-chah, his x mark,

No-wo-ko, his x mark,

Win-in-a-pa, his x mark,

Oke-lah-shah-cubbe, his x mark,

Ish-ta-ki-yu-ka-tubbe, his x mark,

Mah-te-ko-shubbe, his x mark,

Tom-chick-ah, his x mark,

Ei-o-che-tubbe, his x mark,

Nuck-sho-pubbe, his x mark,

Fah-lah-mo-tubbe, his x mark,

Co-chub-be, his x mark,

Thomas Sely, his x mark,

Oke-lah-sha-pi-a, his x mark,

Signed and sealed in the presence of

Ben. Reynolds, *Indian agent,*

George Wightman, *of Mississippi,*

John L. Allen, *subagent,*

John Donley, *Tennessee,*

Nath. Anderson, *secretary to the commissoner,*

D.S. Parrish, *Tennessee,*

S. Daggett, *Mississippi,*

Benj. Love, *United States interpreter,*

Wm. A. Clurm,

Robert Gordon, *Mississippi,*

G. Long.

(a) This treaty appears not to have been ratified. The original is on file in the Indian Office (Box 1, Treaties, 1802-1853) and a copy is found in the appendix, post p. 1035

In 1836, Edmund Pickens gathered his growing family, which included his wife and many relatives, and began a journey involving unimaginable struggles. Their destination was Indian Territory – the new land to be occupied by his tribe for centuries to come.

This long, difficult journey that came to be known as the "Trail of Tears," was under the direction of Chickasaw Agent A. M. M. Upshaw, who had been appointed by U.S. officials. Starting at their home in the most northern part of the original Chickasaw territory, they traveled west until they came to the Mississippi River. Thousands of Chickasaws were gathered at one of the Chickasaw Bluffs, now known as the city of Memphis, Tennessee. Although this was one of the widest points of the river, it was a central crossing point for Chickasaws. The majority of Chickasaws were ferried across this section of the river by U.S. boats.

At that time, the Mississippi River was one of the most magnificent spectacles in the world. Its banks were teaming with enormous pines and oaks, the water was murky and fast and the opposite shore was a great distance away. This posed a dangerous problem for the people, because in addition to entire families needing to cross the river, there were thousands of horses, livestock, pets, wagons and buggies filled with invaluable possessions – all these things had to be ferried across.

Crossing the Mississippi River was a monumental and sometimes deadly task. In an earlier crossing, hundreds of Creek Indians drowned when one of their boats sank. This incident prompted some Chickasaw families to attempt an independent crossing at narrower points south of the Chickasaw Bluffs, near what is now Adams County, Mississippi. Unfortunately, these narrower parts of the river were also dangerous. There were still many Chickasaw casualties and deaths. Some Chickasaws refused to travel by boat until they came to the intersection of the Arkansas River at Skullyville, Indian Territory.

After risking their lives crossing the Mississippi River, Edmund Pickens and his family continued their long, arduous journey through the Arkansas forests, fields and streams. There were many obstacles along the way, but luckily there was no recorded loss of life for the Pickens family. A native of Tennessee, William R. Guy served as an assistant conductor and commissary agent for the removal party. As an agent for the federal government, Guy was sympathetic to the Chickasaws' plight. According to reports sent back to headquarters by Guy, the United States officials failed to fulfill their duty regarding food, clothing and many other supplies promised the tribe at various stations along the way. When thousands of Chickasaws arrived at these locations, they found decaying and molded meat that had not been salted for preservation. The Chickasaw people were looking forward to fresh water and other supplies; however, there were none. At one point, William R. Guy stated he was suffering as much as the Chickasaw emigrants. His letters were extremely critical of the United States government.

At one point the marshes were so deep that thousands of animals became stuck. The Chickasaws were helpless and had to leave their livestock to die in the mud. One man who was returning from the westward part of what is now Arkansas, came upon them and wrote a letter to his family describing the situation.

"Much money could not compensate for the loss of what I have seen. With all, there was mixed sympathy for the exiles – for they go unwillingly – whether it be for their good or not – moreover the agents and officers all concurred in speaking of the integrity of the men and good behavior of the women ... They said that it rarely happened that any violence was committed by them against the whites, but after receiving the worst and strongest provocation ... I do not think that I have ever been a witness of so remarkable a scene as was formed by this immense column of moving Indians ... with the train of Govt. wagons, the multitude of horses; it is said three to each Indian and besides at least six dogs and cats to an Indian. They were all most comfortably clad – the men in complete Indian dress with showy shawls tied in turban fashion round their heads – dashing about on their horses, like Arabs, many of them presenting the finest countenances and figures that I ever saw. The women (were) also very decently clothed like white women, in calico gowns – but much tidier and better put on than common white-people – and how beautifully they managed their horses how proud and calm and erect,

*they sat in full gallop. The young women have remarkably
mild and soft countenances and are singularly decorous
in their dress and deportment ... It was a striking scene
at night – when the multitudes of fires kindled, showed to
advantage the whole face of the country covered with the
white tents and covered wagons, with all the interstices ...
filled with a dense mass of animal life ... the picturesque
looking Indian negroes, with dress belonging to no country
but partaking of all, and these changing and mingling
with hundreds of horses hobbled and turned out to feed
and the troops of dogs chasing about in the search of food
... then you would hear the whoops of Indians calling their
family party together to receive their rations, from another
quarter of a wild song from the negroes preparing the corn,
with the strange chorus that the rest would join in ... this
would set a thousand hounds baying and curs yelping
– and then the fires would catch tall dead trees and rush-
ing to the tops throw a strong glare over all this moving
scene, deepening the savage traits of the men, and softening
the features of the women*

John E. Parsons (ed.), Letters on the Chickasaw Removal of 1837, New
York Historical Society Quarterly, Vol. XXXVII (1953), 273 - 283.

During the removal, many Indians became ill with pneumonia,
smallpox and countless other diseases. Entire families died
and groups of Chickasaws were obliged to stop and bury their
family members. Some of the families, including the Johnstons
and Keels, refused to travel with the large group. Ironically,
this decision may have spared them the same disease and
hardships suffered by the rest of the tribe. Beloved Chickasaw
Chief Tishomingo died at an advanced age in what is now the

Chickasaw Removal by Tom Phillips.
[Image courtesy of the Chickasaw Nation Art Collection]

southwestern part of Arkansas, near Little Rock. He was buried in Arkansas, along with many other Indians—many within unmarked graves.

While traveling, Chickasaws came across various encampments, resulting in relationships and even marriages with the people who were managing the camps. Many of these encampment conductors sent letters by pony to their supervisors and officials of the United States government, describing the horrible situation under which the Chickasaws were being forced to travel. (Most of those letters are now available in United States government files.)

When the Chickasaws arrived at Skullyville ("skully" is a Chickasaw and Choctaw word for money), they encountered the wonderful Arkansas River. At some points, the river was sandy; at other points it was covered with lush foliage. In some places, there were huge cane breaks that the animals fed on. On the Arkansas River, near the town of Little Rock, they disagreed on which way to go. Some followed the river past Skullyville and crossed at what is now the border of Arkansas and Oklahoma. Others went southwest, all the way across Arkansas until they came to the Choctaw settlements. Some Chickasaws stayed there permanently.

Edmund and his family found a beautiful location on a bluff overlooking the Red River in what is now Marshall County, Oklahoma. Ironically, thirty-one years later in 1867, he would be buried in that very place. So at this time and place, Edmund Pickens and his family, along with their many friends and relatives, began a new life in Indian Territory. With a spirit that refused to be conquered, the Chickasaws would soon become one of the most important and respected American Indian tribes in the country.

THE NEW HOME

C H A P T E R S I X

With mixed feelings, Edmund and his family began the task of establishing themselves a home. On one hand, they were grateful for arriving safely at their destination. On the other hand, they were in a new, unfamiliar land and faced many challenges. Fortunately, the family found a lovely location for their home on a bluff overlooking the Red River. The cabins erected by Edmund and the other men were indeed acceptable. Within a few days, all was well with the exhausted family. Attempting to put aside the hardships endured during their recent journey, they made plans for the future.

The scenery surrounding their new home was stunning. On the south was the magnificent Red River and to the north and east was Rock Creek. A beautiful easterly slope provided a view of neighbors on the riverbanks a mile away, while the western area was lush with vegetation. Edmund Pickens and his family had selected one of the most enviable areas in the new Chickasaw Nation. Life for the Chickasaws at that time promised great hope. Unfortunately, they could not foresee the unbelievable acts awaiting them in the coming years.

As the Pickens family grew, they continued to participate in the affairs of the Chickasaw Nation. The 1839 census of the Chickasaw Nation showed that the Edmund Pickens family had three male children under the age of ten and one male child over the age of ten. There were two adult males between the ages of twenty and forty-nine and one male that was older than fifty years of age. In addition, the census lists the family as having one female child under the age of ten years, three female children over the age of ten years, and one female over age fifty. Also listed were five slaves.

The Pickens family had a relatively happy life together until tragedy struck in 1856. Before the arrival of the Chickasaws, the land Edmund now occupied was a hunting ground for the Comanche Indians. The new Chickasaw occupation had created conflicts between the two tribes, even to the point of actual battles. It was during a battle between the Chickasaws and the Comanches somewhere near what is presently McMillan, Chickasaw Nation, that Edmund's sons Johnson and David were shot by poisoned arrows. Johnson's wound was fatal, while David survived.

The death of Edmund's oldest son Johnson was devastating. Johnson was buried in Graveyard Bluff near the family's home. His burial was according to Chickasaw custom, and his funeral service was similar to what was usually held for a chief's family member. Through the years, many other Pickens family members were buried in that cemetery, including Edmund himself.

In his book *The Indians of the Southeastern United States*, John R. Swanton made the following observation concerning Chickasaw funerals of the 18th century:

"As soon as death occurred firebrand was dropped into the water. [Bernard] Romans made the following statement. The house fire was extinguished and a new fire started. Guns were discharged and howls raised to drive away ghosts or as a signal to the relatives. A frame of white sticks was placed on the doorway where a household was mourning and the mourners had a lock of hair clipped off the deceased's body and refrained from salt foods. When a warrior died, drums and musical instruments were laid aside for three days while the body was washed, anointed, dressed in the best clothes the deceased had possessed and seated outside facing the door of the winter house. It was borne around the winter house three times and afterwards seated in the grave facing east with the arms and other moveable property the departed had possessed in life ar- ranged around it. Thick logs were then laid over the tomb covered in turn with cypress bark and clay and the living often slept near the gravesite--particularly the widow or widower of the deceased. Those who performed the last rites must be cleansed, button snake root being used as a medicine and they went around their usual task in three days while the relations mourned for a long time and cried at the grave. In rocky country it was common for a pass- erby to throw stones on the grave of one who had died far from home."

Bernard Romans was born in the Netherlands and lived from 1720-1784. He was a navigator, surveyor, cartographer, naturalist, engineer, soldier, promoter and writer. He is best known for his book published in 1775, *A Concise Natural History of East and West Florida.* In it he describes many of the traditional lifeways of Southeastern Indian populations.

INDIAN TERRITORY

C H A P T E R   S E V E N

The original Indian settlement for the Chickasaws was actually the western half of the new Choctaw territory. The Choctaws and Chickasaw have a deep and historic relationship. In fact, they were once the same tribe before their original migration to the Mississippi area. The two tribes frequently intermarried and upheld a natural social code. In fact, no fences existed between properties. When cattle, horses and other livestock became intermingled, the owners would report to each other as soon as possible. Livestock and properties were quickly returned to their rightful owners.

At that time, the northern portion of Texas along the Red River was heavily populated with white settlers. Surrounded by white settlers and the aforementioned Indian tribes, the Chickasaws built their new homes and lived their lives as best they could – even if there was an occasional conflict. The first 20 years were what was to be expected for a tribe moving into what was complete wilderness. Although the Chickasaws continued their laws and customs, there was much to contend with.

Of course, conflicts did occur between the Chickasaws and Choctaws. One serious event involved David Pickens, son of Edmund Pickens. David was a Chickasaw Light Horseman, which meant that he was charged with upholding the law for the Chickasaw Nation. One day he caught a Choctaw man carrying a huge amount of liquor across the Red River from North Texas. This type of contraband was illegal in Indian Territory. When David confronted the man, the Choctaw drew a weapon and David was forced to protect himself. The man eventually died from his wounds. This caused quite a stir between the two tribes. However, David was only doing his job.

With a shared history and now shared land, the two tribes signed the Treaty of Doaksville in 1837, resulting in a united Choctaw/Chickasaw government. The Chickasaws paid $530,000 to the Choctaws for the right to settle in their lands. Ishtehotopa was the active Chickasaw Chief at this time. Edmund was the elected Tribal Treasurer and Second Controlling Chief. (It should be noted that Edmund was skilled in financial matters. He managed his own financial conditions quite well and as Tribal Treasurer, he assumed financial responsibility for the tribe.)

"For the purpose of dividing their annuities, the Chickasaw Nation had been divided into four companies back in Mississippi, headed by Tishomingo, McGilvery, Albertson and Thomas Seeley. Edmund Pickens was now (1845) appointed second controlling chief to act as treasurer and handle all of the tribal funds. Pitman Colbert wrote Superintendent Armstrong of the recent council and said, 'we have placed our friend Edmund Pickens in the same situation as my old

uncle Levi Colbert was in the old Chickasaw Nation.' He added that his uncle was impoverished by the great number of Indians that had visited him and were fed at his table. Pickens would have similar calls upon his hospitality and it was hoped that a salary would be provided so that he might be able to assume the burden. Armstrong refused to recognize the officers chosen and paid it to the individual citizens as usual. He expressed himself deeply interested in their plans for a manual labor school projected by the Methodist Church, for the Chickasaws were in a better position to provide for education than most of the Indian tribes."

~ The Oklahoma Historical Society's *Chronicles of Oklahoma*

Edmund Pickens exhibited some of the finest qualities known to man: honesty, integrity, high moral values and common sense.

After removal, Edmund's presence was consistently requested for business trips between Indian Territory and Washington, D.C. It is important to remember that communication surrounding the Chickasaw Nation, including trips to and from Washington, D.C. were difficult. Travel was limited to horseback, buggy, surrey, wagon or just plain walking. On the way to Washington, D.C., houses owned by private citizens served as accommodations for Chickasaw tribal officials. On one occasion, Edmund accompanied two officials to Washington, D.C. for urgent tribal business. Not knowing exactly what this trip would entail, the tribal officials gave Edmund a blank check. They knew that the business on that trip would be handled with all honesty and trustworthiness.

Edmund also signed for payment of salaries and expenses negotiated with the Choctaw tribe in 1833. The negotiation rate would have been $1,440.00. It was signed by Sampson Folsom, Edmund Pickens, Benjamin Love, (delegates) and Aaron V. Brown, Interpreter.

The following are examples of transactions:

Edmund Pickens signed a disbursement in 1833 for $6.00. "I certify on honor that the above is complete and just and that I have paid the amount thereof." Signed by I. Miller.

Reference from Diplomats in Buckskin: By Herman J. Uida, page 157-158.

Two separate rooms, fire, lights, extra servant and attention for the following persons, delegates of the Choctaw, Chickasaw, and Cherokee Nations, while sick at the Washington House, during the months of February, March and April 1866, and the consequent loss of articles of bedding and c. Colonel Adair, sick with smallpox about four weeks his bill was $190.00. Mr. Mitchell sick with smallpox about 20 days $60. Robert Love, sick with smallpox three weeks $63.

Governor Colbert, sick with pneumonia six weeks – $135. 00

Governor Wade, sick with pneumonia five weeks – $112.00

Governor Pickens, two separate rooms – $30.00

Two large hair mattresses – $70.00

1 small hair mattress – $25

4 feather pillows – $10.00

and four cases – $10.00

5 sheets – $10.00

2 blankets – $20.00

2 comforts – $15.00

6 towels – $3.00

Beverages received $500 of the $673 they requested.

❁

In 1847, Chief Ishtehotopa became gravely ill. Efforts by the Chickasaw medicine men to save the Chief failed and he eventually died. Ishtehotopa had no sons and was unable to pass on his leadership in the traditional manner. Being the Tribal Treasurer and Second Controlling Chief, Edmund had the respect and trust of practically every Chickasaw citizen. Thus, upon the death of long-time Chickasaw Chief Ishtehotopa, Edmund became the first elected Chickasaw Chief.

"A document provided for an executive to be appointed by the Chickasaw Council, with the title of Chickasaw District Chief; and a council of thirty members to meet on the first Monday of October. A general council was held immediately after the adoption of the 1848 constitution. The first Chickasaw Chief to be elected under this new constitution was Edmund Pickens."

~ The Oklahoma Historical Society's *Chronicles of Oklahoma*

The names of the captains, elected and appointed at Boiling Springs in July 1847 were Sloan Love, Ishtochock, Ishtochockathla, Isaac Albertson, Jackson Frasier, Winchester Colbert, Ahfahmah, Ishhoiyowkatubby, Chickasaw Nahnubby, William Newberry, James Wolf, Mahyahtubby, Thomas Seeley, William James, Edmund Pickens, ?? Lewis, Ship ?? Howwa, Mah hotiche, Mkiyea, Ahmishotubby, Terry ?, Shyahkahhubby, Shbelonmoyah, Oklahnahmubby and Tshlaholopa.

Pittman Colbert delivered the official nomination and Edmund Pickens assumed the office of Chickasaw Tribal Chief with the full confidence of the Chickasaw people. Despite previous hardships, the new chief and his family continued their lives with confidence and hope.

Edmund's tenure as chief covered a period of time that was critical in the history of the Chickasaw Nation. With all the changes the Chickasaws had to endure during the first half of the eighteenth century, they were lucky to have a leader as skilled as Edmund.

The Chickasaw Nation has always been known for their leadership qualities. One of the most well-known men during the tribe's move to the west was Benjamin Love. He was the grandson of James Logan Colbert, the Scotsman who had settled with the tribe as a young man, was married to Chickasaw women and had several children. James Logan Colbert's first two wives were full-blooded Chickasaws. After they died, James remarried and had several more children with Chickasaw half-bloods, one of which was Benjamin. Benjamin, who was brilliant, educated and talented in many ways, was a natural leader. He was highly respected and tribal members often sought him out for aid in Chickasaw business concerns. The Love family had lived only a few miles west of the Pickens family in Mississippi, and Edmund was well acquainted with Benjamin Love.

Benjamin's sudden death at the hands of a Shawnee tribal member was a tragic occasion for the Chickasaw Nation. In her book *Chickasaw Loves and Allied Families*, Marie Garland stated that Ben Love was killed on July 3, 1849, at Houani Creek, north of what is now Lebanon, Oklahoma. He was 54 years old. A Shawnee man stated that two Chickasaw men had hired him to kill Benjamin Love, but this was never proven.

As a child, my mother, Lula Potts Keel, relayed a different story to me. She stated that the two men who killed Benjamin Love were Adam Jemmie and Raven Porter. They were held in custody for a long time, but were eventually set free. Someone killed Porter as he crossed the Red River. Adam Jemmie was killed near the Adam Jemmie Point (Jimmey).

In Edmund's attempt to seek federal prosecution for Benjamin's murderer, he wrote the following letter to the Secretary of the Interior, Thomas Ewing:

Fort Washitaw C. N.
August 17, 1849.

Hon. Thomas Ewing, Secretary of Interior –

Dear Sir –

We would most respectfully inform you that we have got difficulties from which it seems almost impossible to extricate ourselves; and in the absence of any one to direct us in matters of importance, we have thought that it would be wise, and we hope not improper to avail ourselves of your superior wisdom and experience, in matters which involve the welfare of our people. Our ignorance of the principles of law, and the high position you occupy as a statesman, we hope will be a sufficient excuse for our asking your advice in this hour of trial.

You perhaps have heard of the assassination of Benjamin Love, a very prominent man of this tribe, by a Shawnee, whom we now have in custody at Fort Washitaw. He acknowledges his guilt, and also implicates two Chickasaws, by whom he said he was hired to commit the murder. While we are satisfied of the guilt of the prisoner, the many conflicting statements made by him concerning his accomplices, if he had any, constrain us to doubt whether or not he is endeavoring to secure the punishment of innocent men. Thus the matter stands after a thorough investigation. Now we desire to deal out justice to all parties. We believe the Shawnee is guilty – no one pretends to deny that – and justice demands that he should be punished; but the Creek nation interferes, and says if we punish him, we must also

punish those who he has implicated, or war will be the con-
sequence; but if we punish those who he implicates, difficulties will certainly arise among the Chickasaws, and scenes
will be enacted which it is painful to contemplate – a system
of assassination, discord and bloodshed will be carried on for
the next five years to come, and what we wish you to decide is,
whether we should permit crime to go on unpunished, or punish men who can establish their innocence beyond a doubt, and
thereby inflict a wound in our own nation which will require
years to heel [sic], in order to keep at peace with a neighboring
nation. This is a subject on which we desire to be enlightened
by your superior wisdom. We appeal to you because we know no
other source. We have an agent here, it is true, but we might as
well have none at all, for he is no use to us – so far from it, he
is a burden upon the shoulders of our people. We have appealed
to him in this as well as other instances, but he will give us no
advice, and the disregard he evinces on all occasions for the
welfare of our people, constrains to the belief that he is not our
true friend.

The man before alluded to as the murderer of Mr. Love, is one
who should not be permitted to run at large, as he confesses
assignation to be his trade - - the means by which he supports
himself, and if he goes unpunished, others of our people may
share the same fate of Mr. Love.

With great respect and esteem, we remain your, &c

his

Edmund Pickens

Mark

Chief Chickasaw

District C. W.

Robt W Nail

District attorney

Cyrus Harris

Clerk. C. District

C.W.

(OIA: Chickasaw File P. 341. Ft. Washita. 1849.)

At the time of his death, Benjamin had been living in the eastern part of what was Love County, Chickasaw Nation, Indian Territory. His grave is located near Marshall County, Oklahoma, a short distance from the western border of that county. Edmund Pickens and Benjamin Love now lie in graves that are near each other.

When the Choctaw and Chickasaw Nations were combined, a somewhat democratic system of government was used. Unfortunately, the Choctaws outnumbered the Chickasaws three-to-one, and the voting often fell along those same lines. Over the years, the Chickasaws became increasingly frustrated with their lack of independence. In 1855,

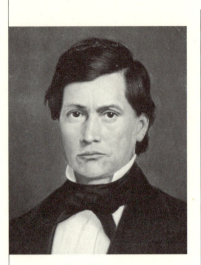

Cyrus Harris, by Juanita Tate, courtesy of the Chickasaw Council House Museum.

Jackson Kemp, by Juanita Tate, courtesy of Juanita Tate collection.

they signed a treaty with the Choctaws that separated the two tribes. A line dividing the tribal properties was surveyed and the Chickasaws assumed separate ownership of the properties west of that line.

After the treaty of 1855 was executed, the Chickasaws decided to formally change their system of government. It would be fully democratic, modeled after the United States system with its three branches: Executive, Legislative and Judicial. This also meant there would be regular elections. In 1856, at Tishomingo, Chickasaw Nation, large numbers of Chickasaw men gathered and concluded that a constitution would be created, voted on and accepted by a Chickasaw Constitution Committee. The first governor elected to serve his Chickasaw people in this capacity was young Cyrus Harris, my great-great grandfather. Cyrus had served as interpreter and clerk during the Chickasaw business transactions back in the old homeland and at the time of the great removal. Jackson Kemp, brother-in-law of Cyrus Harris, was chairman of this convention and Edmund Pickens was elected as a member of the new Chickasaw Legislature.

The 1856 Constitutional Convention was composed of the following representatives:

Jackson Kemp, President of the Convention
Attest: Geo. D. James, Secretary of the Convention

A.V. Brown	D. Colbert
Sampson Folsom	Henry McKinney
Wm. Simpson	Capt. Jerry
Ar Chanah Tuby	Capt. Lewis
Benjamin Maytuby	Pesubby
Benjamin S. Love	James Patterson
Cyrus Harris	Joel Kemp
James Gamble	Capt. Ned
Martin Shecoe	Capt. Wilson Frazier
Lemuel Colbert	Capt. Hoytubby
Morgan Colbert	Capt. Hothli Cha
Robert Love	Capt. T.F. Anderson
F.M. McLish	Capt. Emoshi Oha
E Me Hutt Tubby	Capt. Emar Ho Ti Cha
E Lah Noon Tubby	Capt. G.W. Allen
Joseph Colbert	Capt. Pis Um Oun Tubby
Im Mun Tubby	Capt. John Parker
Winchester Colbert	Capt. E Lap Am Bee

Christopher Columbus	James N. M'Lish
Own Ut Ubby	Sam'l Colbert
Edmund Pickens	John M. Johnson
A. Alexander	William Kemp
Horace Pratt	

Edmund Pickens did his duty well in that regard. He continued to be known for his honesty and integrity, and would go out of his way to help his fellow Chickasaws. During smallpox epidemics in Washington D.C., he helped where he could. Oddly enough, he never fell victim to that disease himself. Simply put, Edmund did what he had to do to help his people. Such was the reputation of Edmund Pickens – the highest quality of character and strong leadership.

When the War Between the States broke out, the Chickasaw Nation chose to side with the Confederate South. Until that time, the United States Government had fallen so far behind in their treaty obligations, the tribe felt their only recourse was to join the Confederacy. Edmund was chosen to sign the treaty between the Chickasaws and the Confederate States of America, along with five other Chickasaws and several Choctaws, including Choctaw Chief Robert M. Jones. On May 25, 1861, Edmund joined the rest in signing this treaty.

As the war progressed, a conflict, that was later called the Battle of Honey Springs, occurred in eastern Indian Territory. The battle changed the course of the war in the Trans-Mississippi West. Fort Smith was captured by the Union as it attempted to reassert its authority over Indian

Territory. Rather than putting an end to the rebellion, their efforts only served to harden Indian Confederate troops in the area. By the end of the war, Chickasaw infrastructure was vitually destroyed. Fourteen percent of of all children in the territory were orphans and 33% of women were widows.

Unfortunately, after the South lost the war and surrendered in 1865, the United States nullified all past treaties with the Chickasaw Nation, leaving the tribe severely crippled. At the end of the Civil War, Chickasaw and Choctaw warriors were compelled to lay down their arms following the invasion of enemy troops. Forced to comply, Edmund Pickens became the first signatory of a new treaty between the Chickasaws, the Choctaws and the United States of America in 1866.

Those signing the treaty on behalf of the Chickasaw Nation were Winchester Colbert, Edmund Pickens, Holmes Colbert, Colbert Carter and Robert Love. The members of the Choctaw delegation who signed were Allen Wright, Alfred Wade, James Riley and John Page.

Of the large number of Chickasaws who had participated in the defense of Chickasaw tribal boundaries, Edmund was foremost in protecting Chickasaw families and helping Chickasaws whose needs came to his attention. It has been said that most of the money he received from the sale of his property in Mississippi was spent assisting Chickasaw friends and relatives. When Edmund died, he was not a wealthy man.

Graveyard Bluff, final resting place of Edmund Pickens.

✹

During the War, Edmund Pickens contracted a serious illness while traveling with a company of Chickasaws in what is now western Carter County. At the time, they were defending Chickasaw territory from several other tribes. An assistant took care of him until he was able to return to the Chickasaw headquarters in northwest Carter County. After the War, in 1868, the illness again struck Edmund. Unfortunately, this time he was unable to defeat the illness and Edmund Pickens passed away. The Chickasaw Nation had lost a true leader.

Surviving him were his wife, Euthlike, and his children: Maulsie Pickens Keel, Iahunta Pickens, Sally Pickens Lavers, Winey Pickens Keel (who insisted being known by her father's

The Pickens and Keel members of the Keel Cemetery Association.

name, Okchantubby), Thomson Pickens and Millie Pickens
McLish. Edmund's estate was probated in 1873, and Robert
Boyd was the attorney over the estate.

Edmund Pickens was buried on the grounds of his longtime
home, now known as Graveyard Bluff, alongside other family
members, including his son Johnson.

When the Denison Dam was built in 1944, it created Lake Tex-
oma. As a result, Graveyard Bluff and its cemetery became an
island. Sadly, many tombstones of the graves surrounding Edmund Pickens have been either stolen or removed. In 2003, my
son, Charles Tate, chairman of the Keel Cemetery Association,
and his son, Ryan Tate, relocated the remaining headstones
from Graveyard Bluff to the Keel Cemetery. Keel Cemetery is
located approximately seven miles north of Edmund Pickens'
Chickasaw allotment land. Johnson Pickens' headstone now

Euthlike Pickens' tombstone located at Keel Cemetery.

lies next to his mother's headstone, Euthlike Pickens, at the Keel Cemetery.

Euthlike Pickens died in 1885 and is buried in the Keel Cemetery near her children Thompson, Winey and Millie. Other Pickens children are now buried in cemeteries a few miles away, not far from Euthlike and Johnson's monuments. Euthlike's tombstone inscription reads: "Erected by Thompson Pickens in memory of my beloved mother who died November 25, 1885 aged about 70 yrs."

The Children of Edmund and Euthlike Pickens:

Johnson Pickens

David Pickens

Mary Jane Pickens

Rachael Pickens

Thompson Pickens

Iahunta Pickens

Alice Pickens

Winey "Winnie" Pickens "Okchantubby"

Millie Pickens

Maulsie Pickens

Descendants have held memorial services for our Pickens family the Sunday preceding Memorial Day for more than 50 years.

Johnson Pickens' tombstone located at Keel Cemetery.

EPILOGUE

I hope that my having written this book will encourage all Chickasaws to begin – or if you have begun, to continue – researching the history of our beloved tribe. Most importantly, I would ask the reader to instill into the minds of our young tribal members the importance of our heritage. This book only chronicles one man's life during the removal to our current homeland. There is still so much more to learn.

Each time I traveled to the old Chickasaw Nation east of the Mississippi River, I made fascinating new discoveries. Hopefully, that territory will be visited again and again by a new generation of Chickasaws. I believe each trip back to the "old country" yields more clues to our past. From the East Coast of the United States to the great Mississippi River, through the hunting grounds of our ancestors – visiting these sites will help preserve our historical past.

I hope you enjoyed reading this brief history of Edmund Pickens as much as I enjoyed creating it. Through our past, we can chart a course for our future – a future that is indeed bright for the Chickasaw Nation.